THE GILL HISTORY OF IRELAND

General Editors: James Lydon, Ph.D
               Margaret MacCurtain, Ph.D.

Other titles in the series

IRELAND IN THE TWENTIETH CENTURY

John A. Murphy

GILL AND MACMILLAN

Published in Ireland by
Gill and Macmillan Ltd
Goldenbridge
Dublin 8
with associated companies in
Auckland, Dallas, Delhi, Hong Kong,
Johannesburg, Lagos, London, Manzini,
Melbourne, Nairobi, New York, Singapore,
Tokyo, Washington
© John A. Murphy, 1975
7171 0568 7
Print origination in Ireland by
Cahill and Co. Ltd, Dublin
Printed in Hong Kong

To Cita

Contents

Foreword

THE study of Irish history has changed greatly in recent decades as more evidence becomes available and new insights are provided by the growing number of historians. It is natural, too, that with each generation new questions should be asked about our past. The time has come for a new large scale history. It is the aim of the Gill History of Ireland to provide this. This series of studies of Irish history, each written by a specialist, is arranged chronologically. But each volume is intended to stand on its own and no attempt has been made to present a uniform history. Diversity of analysis and interpretation is the aim; a group of young historians have tried to express the view of their generation on our past. It is the hope of the editors that the series will help the reader to appreciate in a new way the rich heritage of Ireland's history.

JAMES LYDON, PH.D.

MARGARET MACCURTAIN, PH.D.

Preface

It has become the custom for an author to draw attention in the preface to his manifest inadequacies. Without indulging in this curious form of self-disparagement, I may be allowed to point out the peculiar difficulties of writing a brief survey of modern, not to say contemporary, Irish history. In the absence of both perspective and documentation, it is obvious that analysis and assessment can only be tentative. As well, a short compass compounds the risks of simplification. Again, no Irishman writing about his own time can honestly claim to be academically remote from it all: he must try to be fair but he cannot escape feeling involved. Finally, I am acutely conscious that every politically-aware Irishman (which is to say, virtually everybody I know) will have his own strong views about the period with which I deal here. Yet the various hazards do not diminish the unique excitement which a historian feels in using, so to speak, living material and in combining contemporary observation with the analysis born of professional experience.

I have set out to give a balanced and readable account of Irish history since 1918. In doing so, I have constantly kept in mind the needs of the student and the general reader who want a compact blend of events and comment and who may not have the opportunity to come to grips at the moment with the more detailed studies discussed in the bibliographical note.

Ireland in the Twentieth Century is not, of course, a chronologically precise description of a book which begins with the events of 1918, but it is arguable that the nineteenth century in Ireland extends at least up to that year.

I owe the reader one or two other explanations. 'Catholic' and 'Protestant' are such convenient and tragically valid terms that I can only express my regret if my use of them offends anybody's susceptibilities. I have frequently used 'Ireland', 'the Irish people', 'the Irish government' when referring to nationalist Ireland or to the Twenty-six Counties after 1922. This is again simply a matter of convenience and does not connote aggressive irredentism. Similarly, 'South' and 'North', as I use them, may not meet with universal approval but they have the merit of simplicity. In all cases, I should hope that the context makes for clarity.

I am particularly indebted to all those who have already ventured courageously into the danger zone of contemporary Irish history. It is a pleasure to acknowledge the kindly help of my friend and general editor, Dr Margaret MacCurtain. I must also salute Ray O'Farrell and Hubert Mahony of Gill and Macmillan for their encouragement and patience.

JOHN A. MURPHY
University College
Cork

1 The Independence Struggle, 1919-21

As the great European war moved towards its bloody climax, nationalist Ireland turned increasingly towards new leaders and policies. However, there was nothing inevitable about the Sinn Féin victory of 1918, nor did the events of the following years stem inevitably from that victory. The successful reconstitution of Sinn Féin in 1917 was accomplished only after various setbacks had been overcome, and even then nobody could have predicted with certainty that the Irish parliamentary party, discredited though it was, would soon be virtually destroyed. In fact, that party's triumph in three by-elections in early 1918 might conceivably have heralded its recovery had not the course of events greatly favoured Sinn Féin and so helped to harden into remarkable electoral support that potential sympathy for the self-declared heirs of the 1916 insurgents which had existed since the popular revulsion at the executions.

From the beginning of 1918 Sinn Féin clubs continued to be established and the Volunteer movement to be strengthened, both functioning overtly. Yet there was no thought of staging another rebellion. Indeed, Volunteers were expected not to use arms and to adopt an attitude of passive resistance. But it was difficult for the Sinn Féin executive and the headquarters staff of the Volunteers to exercise any firm control over the actions of local units, and local independence of central control was to be a significant feature of the following years. It was common practice for Volunteers to raid private houses for guns, contrary to the strict orders of the Executive, and even in the first half of 1918 there were isolated attacks on policemen and raids on barracks.

Meanwhile the Irish Convention (Lloyd George's attempt to settle the Irish question through a conference of all shades of opinion) was drawing to an ineffectual close, having foundered on the rocks of Sinn Féin abstention and Ulster Unionist intransigence. Its final report, signed by less than half the members on 5 April 1918, envisaged a limited form of Home Rule. A committee of the Convention warned against imposing compulsory military service on Ireland, as did a message in April to the British government from President Wilson who expressed concern about probable Irish-American reaction. Yet the military men pressed the cabinet to apply conscription to Ireland. It was true, of course, that not for generations had there been so many young men in Ireland, kept at home by the stoppage of emigration, the wartime farming prosperity and the excitement of a nationalist resurgence. Those who had a mind to do so were already in military service and any astute government should have realised that, anti-British feeling apart, the reluctant ones would find total resistance to conscription, no matter what its outcome, preferable to inglorious death in Flanders. Yet once again good sense deserted an English government in its dealings with Ireland.

Early in April Lloyd George introduced a bill empowering the government to enforce conscription. The promise of a Home Rule measure did not make the conscription bill more palatable to the Irish Parliamentary Party who strongly opposed it and who, following its passage, withdrew from Westminster to organise resistance at home. After John Redmond's death in March, John Dillon became the new – and last – leader of the party. Anti-conscription was now the great issue in Ireland. At a conference in the Mansion House in Dublin, attended by leading members of the Irish party, Sinn Féin, Labour and other groups, an anti-conscription pledge was drawn up by which people should 'pledge ourselves solemnly to one another to resist conscription by the most effective means at our disposal'. The Catholic bishops, at the prompting of Eamon de Valera, publicly condemned the conscription proposal. The pledge was widely signed on Sunday 21 April and a one-day general strike was observed on 23 April. It is significant that although the resistance to conscription was on an all-party basis the credit was reaped by Sinn Féin and de Valera who had drawn up the pledge and who were most associated in the popular mind with the campaign.

The popularity of Sinn Féin was further strengthened by the 'German plot' episode. The Dublin Castle authorities announced that 'certain subjects of . . . the King, domiciled in Ireland, have conspired to enter into . . . treasonable communication with the German enemy'. The 'plot', it was hoped, would discredit Sinn Féin leaders in American eyes and weaken the anti-conscription campaign. In mid-May nearly all the leading Sinn Féin and Volunteer organisers including de Valera and Arthur Griffith – but not Collins who evaded capture – were arrested and deported to England, there to be interned. At the same time, no evidence was produced which might incriminate the arrested persons. The arrests were followed by considerable police activity against public meetings while Sinn Féin, the Volunteers, Cumann na mBan and the Gaelic League were all proclaimed as dangerous associations. There was extensive popular defiance of these measures, and support for Sinn Féin was firmly shown in the East Cavan by-election in June 1918 when the imprisoned Griffith triumphed over his Irish party opponent.

As the Volunteers, now numbering over 100,000, prepared to resist any attempt to impose conscription, the government hesitated to issue the order-in-council which would bring the measure into force at once. The conclusion of the armistice on 11 November 1918 put an end to the controversial issue but not to its far-reaching effects on Irish politics. Already the conscription threat had resulted in the Irish party's withdrawal from Westminster – and thus in the effective end of parliamentarianism – and in an invaluable boost to Sinn Féin which had so successfully exploited the conscription issue. More than

3

any other development, conscription put paid to moderation and to the hopes of an agreed settlement. For the British government there were no compensating factors; Churchill was to observe ruefully that 'we had the worst of both worlds, all the resentment against compulsion and in the end no law and no men'.

The war was over but there was little likelihood of the immediate granting of Home Rule. Ulster was not to be coerced, Home Rule with an exclusion of the north was unacceptable even to moderate nationalist opinion and, in any case, Sinn Féin was demanding much more than a modest measure of self-government. A general election was now imminent, the first to test the mood of the electorate since 1910, and that electorate was a dramatically increased one. The Representation of the People Act, 1918, can be considered as the culmination of the long process of broadening the basis of parliamentary representation by breaking the link between property and the franchise, to achieve universal suffrage. The parliamentary vote was now extended on the basis of age (21) and six months' residence. The full demands of the suffragists were not conceded but women over the age of thirty were given the vote, though they still had to be local government electors or the wives of these electors. The enfranchisement of women, even on a partial basis, was bound to enhance the prospects of Sinn Féin since women had been extremely active in the movement, especially in the crucial period between the 1916 Rising and the reconstitution of Sinn Féin in 1917. In other respects, the Act improved the existing electoral system but its main achievement was the creation of a large and diversified electorate which was bound to affect permanently the whole complexion of British and Irish politics.

A comparison between the register in the 1910 election and the revised register under the 1918 Act speaks eloquently for itself. The Irish electorate as a whole jumped from 701,475 to 1,936,673, Dublin City increasing from 35,353 voters to 124,829, Belfast from 57,174 to 170,901, Cork from 12,296 to 45,017, Limerick from 4,875 to 17,121 and Waterford from 2,972 to 12,063. It has been estimated

4

that two-thirds of those on the 1918 register were about to vote for the first time. Here was an enormous potential for change. Even if revolutionary nationalism had not been in the ascendant, it was very likely that vast masses of new voters, many of them young and poor, would still be ready for political adventure, or at least for some change in the *status quo*.

The enlarged electorate and the emergence of a new party ended the stagnation that had characterised Irish elections for a generation. The majority of seats in an Irish general election had not been contested since 1892; in the December 1910 election 60 constituencies were uncontested. Between that election and 1918 there had been thirty-one by-elections, nineteen of which had returned unopposed candidates. Set against these figures, the uncontested election of 25 Sinn Féin candidates out of a total of 105 constituencies in 1918 should be seen as striking evidence of the liveliness of political activity in this dramatic post-war election and not as an indication of political indifference, which has sometimes been the interpretation of this statistic.

Although the Parliamentary party polled a quarter of a million votes, this was of little importance in a total electorate of almost two million. The party which had dominated nationalist politics since the 1880s and which had 80 seats at the beginning of 1918 was now reduced to a pathetic remnant. Of the six seats it retained, four were in Ulster constituencies where Sinn Féin and the party had agreed not to split the anti-Unionist vote. Nationalist Ireland had decisively rejected parliamentarianism: what it wanted in its place was not perhaps quite so clear.

Twenty-six Unionists were returned, all but three of them in north-east Ulster. Sinn Féin secured 73 of the 105 seats. Intimidation and personation undoubtedly took place but were not confined to any one party and did not seriously affect the outcome. Besides, Sinn Féin fought the election under serious handicaps; its members were the object of hostile attention from police and military, its election manifesto was censored and more than half its candidates were in jail – though this latter fact was perhaps more a political asset than a liability. Its share of the total poll – 47.7 per cent of all votes cast – did not really reflect Sinn Féin strength in nationalist Ireland since it included the dominant Unionist areas of the north-east: it is more realistic to consider that it secured almost 65 per cent of the vote cast in the contested constituencies of what afterwards came to be called 'the Twenty-six counties '.

A remarkable electoral triumph, then, it certainly was, and this was conceded by the *Freeman's Journal*, which had long supported the Irish party, as well as by *The Times* which spoke of Sinn Féin's 'overwhelming' victory: 'The General Election in Ireland was treated by all parties as a plebiscite and admittedly Sinn Féin swept the country'.

But how are we to interpret the mandate given by the nationalist electorate? Obviously there was the emphatic rejection of a discredited party, tarred with the brush of partition and the failure to secure Home Rule. The popular vote was also an expression of revulsion at the government's ineptitude in such matters as the 'German plot' and the imprisonment of Sinn Féin members. The vote demonstrated appreciation of Sinn Féin's effective leadership of the anti-conscription campaign, the great rallying point of national emotion in 1918. But there can be little doubt that the principal wish of the nationalist electorate was that Sinn Féin should seek and achieve full independence for Ireland. The organisation had spelt out its policy in unequivocal terms during the election campaign. Its manifesto had declared its objective to be the establishment of a republic, it affirmed support for the 1916 proclamation, asserted 'the inalienable right of the Irish Nation to sovereign independence', promised an end to parliamentarianism and the establishment of a constituent assembly 'as the supreme national authority', and announced that Sinn Féin would appeal to the Peace Conference to support Ireland's claim to be an 'independent nation'. The electorate which so resoundingly endorsed this manifesto was clearly looking for Irish independence in a form and spirit of a kind never envisaged by the Irish party. That the voters were not committed rigidly to a doctrinaire realisation of that independence was equally manifest. De Valera subsequently declared that the vote for Sinn Féin was 'not for a form of government so much, because we are not republican doctrinaires, but . . . for Irish freedom and Irish independence'. For the nationalist in the street as for the Volunteer in combat in the years that followed, the struggle was for the substance of freedom and independence. There was, in short, a flexibility in the national demand: it was neither necessary nor wise to claim that the people had voted uncompromisingly for 'The Republic'.

Early in January 1919 Sinn Féin representatives decided to convene the constituent assembly promised in the manifesto. The successful candidates in *all* Irish constituencies, of whatever political complexion, were invited to take their seats in *Dáil Éireann* (Assembly of Ireland) at its opening session on 21 January. As expected, only the members of parliament elected in the Sinn Féin interest accepted the invitation, and of those only such attended as were not imprisoned or in hiding. Thus only 28 out of a total of 105 Irish members attended the opening meeting of the first Dáil at the Mansion House in Dublin under the presidency of Cathal Brugha, a republican militant of Easter Week fame. During a historic two-hour session the Dáil approved of a provisional constitution, endorsed a declaration of independence, appointed delegates to the Peace Conference, sanctioned a message to the free nations of the world and adopted a 'democratic programme' of social and economic reform.

There are many aspects of that first session, and of the First Dáil generally, that are highly significant. The absence through imprisonment of 'moderate' Sinn Féin leaders like de Valera and Griffith left the field clear for the extremists who expressed the demand for national independence in intransigent republican terms. The members of the Dáil asserted a continuity of objective with the 1916 insurgents and 'did ratify the establishment of the Irish Republic'. The commitment to the 'republic' left little room for compromise in any future negotiations with the Ulster Unionists and the British authorities, as well as sowing the seeds of dissension in Sinn Féin itself. Moreover, a less extreme demand might conceivably have made some headway at the Peace Conference. But the fateful mystique of the 'republic' predated perhaps the first session of Dáil Éireann. It was already implicit in the canonisation of the 1916 men which was an integral part of the new or 'second' Sinn Féin movement and in the formulation of the 1917 Ard-Fheis: 'Sinn Féin aims at securing the international recognition of Ireland as an independent Irish Republic. Having achieved that status the Irish people may by Referendum freely choose their own form of Government'.

But it is also true that the constitution and proceedings of the First Dáil furnish strong evidence of conservatism and continuity. The committee which drafted the constitution adopted by the Dáil included George Gavan Duffy, Seán T. Ó Ceallaigh and Eoin MacNeill, men who certainly could not be classed as extremists. The kind of parliament and executive they envisaged, the relation of legislature to executive, the details of parliamentary procedure – all were within the British parliamentary tradition. Despite the Gaelic nomenclature and the fond notion entertained by some that the new order was 'a return to the idea behind the old Gaelic state', despite the undoubted influence of Gaelic League ideas on the minds of many deputies, Dáil Éireann was essentially modelled on the British form of parliamentary democracy which was, of course, a vital part of Ireland's nineteenth-century heritage.

The lack of any intent to initiate radical *social* change was emphasised by the non-representation of labour and trade union interests in the Dáil. Before 1916, Connolly had made no secret of his contempt for the social conservatism of Sinn Féin. Conversely, Griffith regarded socialism as industrially and politically divisive and feared the danger to the 'national' aim from 'class objectives'. The mutual suspicion persisted in the years after 1916 and Labour

8

feared for its own identity according as Sinn Féin developed into a great national front. Though Labour's national executive resolved in September 1918 to contest the coming general election on an abstentionist basis, there was considerable dissension within the party on the matter. Eventually it was decided to leave a clear field to Sinn Féin and to the issue of self-determination. The decision was to be a fateful one for the political future of Labour.

The members of the First Dáil were, on average, highly-educated, with the professions and the lower levels of the commercial world far better represented than workers and peasants. Yet the Dáil's outlook on social matters was due less to its social composition than to the conservative social climate in Ireland generally, to the Sinn Féin conviction that sectional issues must not endanger the broad national objective of liberation, and also perhaps to the determination that the Dáil's actions must be seen by the watching world to be 'responsible', and far removed from anarchy or bolshevism.

Another indication of the essentially moderate philosophy of Sinn Féin (and of its *political* rather than *revolutionary* outlook) lay in its pre-election arrangement with the Irish party and the Catholic bishops about the marginal constituencies in Ulster. More instructive, however, is a consideration of the circumstances in which the First Dáil came to adopt the Democratic Programme, often mistakenly regarded as a revolutionary social manifesto of a revolutionary body. In fact it was in no way an integral expression of Sinn Féin philosophy but in part a concession to political Labour and the small socialist element in republicanism, and in part a calculated political gesture which could strengthen Labour's claim to full representation at the Berne international socialist conference and thus gain support for Ireland's claim to national independence. IRB members looked askance at the idea of a Democratic Programme, and this attitude was characteristic of a body which traditionally had considered its *raison d'etre* 'to get the English out of Ireland'. It is noteworthy that the original notes for the Programme, the work of Labour

9

leaders Thomas Johnson and William O'Brien, were much more radical in content and tone than the moderate final document prepared by Seán T. Ó Ceallaigh. Even in its diluted form, however, the Programme stood for a policy of extensive social and economic change ('We declare that the nation's sovereignty extends . . . to all its material possessions; the nation's soil and all its resources, all the wealth and all the wealth-producing processes within the nation and . . . we reaffirm that all rights to private property must be subordinated to the public right and welfare.'). Though it was adopted unanimously, it is unlikely that it was given any serious thought at that first euphoric session.

It is very doubtful if revolutionary social doctrines would have found any real sympathy in the rural Ireland of the period. The conservatism bred by peasant proprietorship and by Irish Catholicism was strengthened by the complacency deriving from the high prices of the wartime agricultural economy. But some social unrest was inevitable in these years of political upheaval, manifesting itself less seriously perhaps in the industrial sphere where there were attempts at incipient soviets, than in renewals of land agitation, particularly in the west of Ireland. Already in early 1918 the headquarters staff of the Volunteers had frowned on participation by their men in cattle drives in Connaught and Clare. In June 1920, a Dáil decree, sounding a characteristic note of caution on land agitation, declared: 'That the present time when the Irish people are locked in a life and death struggle with their traditional enemy, is ill-chosen for the stirring up of strife amongst our fellow countrymen; and that all our energies must be directed towards the clearing out – not the occupiers of this or that piece of land – but the foreign invader of our country'.

Some commentators have professed to see a clear social distinction between 'moderate, urban, lower middle class' Sinn Féin and the 'propertyless' Volunteers. It is very doubtful if we can draw such hard and fast lines between the Sinn Féin interest and that of the Volunteers. Few of the latter concerned themselves about social issues – or about constitutional formulae. By and large they would have seen themselves as fighting simply 'to free Ireland': their instinctive assumption was that a free Ireland would be a prosperous and socially just Ireland. Volunteer attacks on the 'Big House' in the 1919–21 period were directed not so much against a privileged social class as against the rump of a garrison ascendancy.

The 1918 election which produced such dramatic consequences in Ireland resulted in Britain in the return of a strongly imperialist parliament. Perhaps there was some relief that the Sinn Féin members did not take their seats at Westminster: Winston Churchill tells us that some Tories had feared an alliance between Sinn Féin and British Labour. Since the convening of the Dáil and its enactments were a clear rejection of British authority in Ireland, how are we to explain British inaction for several months? The answer must lie in such factors as war-weariness, public indifference to Irish affairs, reluctance to create a fresh crop of Irish martyrs, the absence of any positive policy towards Ireland and, as well perhaps, something of a wait-and-see attitude to the Sinn Féin effort to secure international recognition. Even moderate success in this field might have altered the whole course of events.

Seán T. Ó Ceallaigh was appointed the Republican government's envoy in Paris, his main task being to secure admission to the Peace Conference of three Dáil delegates. There was never the remotest chance that he would succeed. The support for Ireland's claim at the Berne Conference and at the Second International at Amsterdam was of little practical use. Backing from the United States would have made a considerable difference but here Anglo-American solidarity remained the insuperable obstacle. As had happened in the Fenian period, Irish-American enthusiasm for the separatist cause made no impact on Washington official policy. President Woodrow Wilson was certainly not going to imperil the special relationship between Britain and America by interfering in what he would regard as the internal business of the United Kingdom. The Friends of Irish Freedom, the Irish-American group which had been formed in 1916, did their utmost to bring pressure to bear on Wilson. A great demonstration of support was evident in the Irish Race Convention at Philadelphia in February 1919, and a Congress resolution in early March expressed sympathy for the Irish cause. This only served to alienate Wilson who was further irritated by the attitudes of the two Clan na Gael leaders, John Devoy and Judge Daniel Cohalan, who expressed pro-German and anti-British sentiments and who were opposed to the President's commitment to the League of Nations ideal. Only with reluctance did Wilson agree to receive a delegation from the Irish Race Convention before he sailed for Europe and then only after Cohalan had been excluded. Wilson remained absolutely unsympathetic to the Irish claim to self-determination and to the question of admitting Irish delegates to the Peace Conference.

On 3 February 1919 de Valera escaped from Lincoln jail and on 1 April was present at the private session of Dáil Éireann which elected him *Priomh–Aire,* the official equivalent in English being 'President', in effect, head of state as well as chief executive. His administration included Arthur Griffith (Home Affairs, and also Deputy President during de Valera's absence in America), Michael Collins (Finance), Cathal Brugha (Defence), Constance Markievicz, the only woman so far elected to the Dáil (Labour) and William Cosgrave (Local Government).

Setting up a legislature and an executive did not, of course, mean that the Republic was really established and flourishing. In some respects the new regime remained merely a *de jure* one. The obstacles it met with were formidable. Its fundamental task was to establish its institutions as an alternative to those of Dublin Castle. Individual members of Dáil Éireann were harassed by the authorities and the assembly itself was suppressed in September 1919. It continued to meet secretly but very infrequently and it transacted little parliamentary business. Its various ministries had to work in circumstances of great difficulty, out of improvised and changing offices and watchful of the unwelcome attention of the police. Nevertheless some of them were remarkably successful.

Perhaps the most important and urgent task facing the Dáil was to find money. Here, as in other departments, the personality of the minister was an important factor in success or failure. Michael Collins, the energetic Minister for Finance, headed the drive to raise a 'Dáil Éireann National Loan' bringing in £358,000. In Local Government, where Cosgrave was ably assisted by Kevin O'Higgins, contacts were being made with councils throughout nationalist Ireland even before the local elections of 1920 which resulted in an impressive victory for Sinn Féin; thereafter, virtually all local bodies switched their allegiance from the Local Government Board to the Dáil Local Government ministry. The Dáil Ministry of Agriculture, under Robert Barton, built up contacts with rural Ireland through a Land Bank which advanced small loans for land purchase and later through a Land Commission which was to extend its activities after independence. But perhaps the most successful aspect of Dáil Éireann's activities was its supplanting of the British machinery of justice, to a large extent, by its own system of 'Dáil Courts' or 'Sinn Féin Courts' which managed to function even when driven underground and whose decisions in various spheres, from land to criminal activity, were frequently implemented by a republican police force.

The original Sinn Féin philosophy would have ruled out an armed struggle for independence. Sinn Féin election speakers in 1918 did not seek a mandate for such a struggle. At least one member of the Dáil, Roger Sweetman, was to have deep misgivings about the drift to a physical force policy and was to resign his seat in January 1921 to indicate his dissent. His unease was shared by many others. There was no definite inception of hostilities; in a sense, the country drifted into increasing terrorism and acts of war. The action which is usually regarded as heralding the opening of the Anglo-Irish war was taken on the very day Dáil Éireann met, and without its knowledge. This was the episode at Soloheadbeg, Co. Tipperary, where two policemen were killed and the gelignite they were escorting seized by Volunteers. The Royal Irish Constabulary were the principal agents of British law and order, their barracks contained the arms and ammunition which the Volunteers needed, and Sinn Féin leaders encouraged republicans to regard the RIC, not as the friendly local figures they often were, but as the eyes and ears of the British presence in Ireland. The police became pathetic casualties of the Anglo-Irish war. While some became brutalised by the atmosphere of terrorism, others felt a desperate conflict of loyalties and many more were simply bewildered by the turn of events, regarding themselves as *Irish* officials doing their duty.

In the struggle which was to mount in intensity up to the 1921 Truce, the Volunteers could feel a sense of legitimacy which was to be denied to their counterparts in other lands later on in the century. They could claim to be the military arm of a political order which had been established by popular vote. They were fighting *within* a democratically established framework and this not only enhanced their own morale but was in part responsible for the support extended to them in their rural 'theatres of war'. But this must not be taken to mean that the Volunteers were subordinate to, or controlled by, Dáil Éireann. The relationship remained a vague and ill-defined one throughout. The Volunteers were in many ways independent of Dáil and Cabinet and, as well as this, tended to act on their own initiative in their own localities without being greatly troubled by control from Volunteer headquarters. Independence of action was enhanced by the lack of agreement among Dáil members and at their own headquarters as to what course Volunteers should pursue.

Cathal Brugha, though Minister for Defence, never had anything like the authority and influence which Michael Collins enjoyed with the Irish Republican Army, as the Volunteers came to be called. Nominally Brugha's subordinate, Collins's various 'military' roles as Adjutant-General, Director of Organisation and Director of Intelligence placed him in a commanding position while as Minister for Finance he was a vital member of the republican cabinet. Between him and Brugha there developed a hostility which was to become public later on. Again, it must be remembered that the IRB continued to exercise a powerful, if as yet undetermined, influence on the course of events down to the Civil War. The fact that some Volunteers were members of the secret brotherhood while others were not was a source not only of confusion but of danger. Brugha, himself an ex-IRB man, was fearful of its influence with the Volunteers and worked to bring the latter under the authority of the Dáil. Collins's prominent membership, and later Presidency, of the Supreme Council made the IRB all the more suspect in Brugha's eyes.

In June 1919 President de Valera began his long sojourn in the United States. Mention has been made of the abortive attempts made to secure President Wilson's help for the Republican cause. In spite of that disappointment, the Sinn Féin leaders considered American help, in terms of financial aid and moral support, to be vital. The President's American mission had the full support of his cabinet. But it was certainly never intended that de Valera should remain away for eighteen months. At the beginning of his visit President Wilson's attitude was beyond doubt, yet de Valera hoped to influence favourably one or both great political parties. He also wished to gain general sympathy for the Irish cause as well as hoping to compose the deep differences which already existed among the leaders of the Irish-American movement. He was to discover for himself a perennial feature of such movements; its leaders had no intention of obeying without question the dictates of nationalist figures from Ireland. Irish-America had its own views on the strategy and tactics of furthering the Irish cause. Though loyally helped by Joseph McGarrity, de Valera fell foul of the two leading figures of the Friends of Irish Freedom, John Devoy and Judge Daniel Cohalan. The quarrel between de Valera and the formidable veterans of the Irish-American political world was partly a personality clash, but it also turned on important policy issues. Even before de Valera's arrival the Friends of Irish Freedom had been divided over the question of whether recognition should be sought for the Irish Republic or simply for Ireland's right to self-determination. McGarrity and others wanted money raised for the Irish cause to be sent directly to Ireland, whereas Devoy and Cohalan believed that most of it should be devoted to promoting Ireland's claim indirectly through activities in America itself. The Devoy-Cohalan group was opposed to de Valera's objective of issuing bonds for the Dáil Éireann loan: in their view floating the loan in the U.S. was impracticable. In the event, de Valera went ahead with the bond drive which was a great success. It realised five million dollars, four million of which were used in Ireland as the indispensable financial sinews of the independence struggle.

The different thinking of Irish-Americans was again indicated on the League of Nations question. Here, they tended to look askance at an organisation which might trap the United States in transatlantic politics and align it with Britain. Apart from fearing that Article X of the Covenant, guaranteeing territorial boundaries, might militate against international recognition of Irish independence, President de Valera had no intrinsic objection to the League. Moreover, he saw no reason why an independent Ireland should not live in amity with a Britain which could be given assurances for its security. His antagonists accused him of compromising the Irish demand for full independence when he propounded the celebrated Cuban analogy in February 1920. Just as Cuba had promised she would not allow herself to be used as a base for attack against the United States, there was no reason why Britain should not 'make a stipulation like this to guard herself against foreign attack'. 'Why doesn't Britain declare a Monroe Doctrine for the two neighbouring islands? The people of Ireland so far from objecting would co-operate with their whole soul'. The proposition was not a realistic one in the circumstances of the time but it prefigured de Valera's ingenious and flexible thinking on constitutional relations in years to come.

The rift between de Valera and the Devoy-Cohalan

faction developed into open hostility. Cohalan and his supporters opposed the President's move at the Republican Party convention to secure recognition of Irish independence as a plank in that party's platform. The attempt to put pressure on the two great American parties – there was a similar move at the Democratic convention – was unwise and, in the event, unsuccessful. But as the President's American tour neared its end, he could look back on triumph as well as on failure. The bond drive was highly successful. There had been the widespread publicity and the enthusiastic receptions which were welcome evidence of American popular support for the Irish cause. On the other hand, the dissensions in Irish-American ranks had been aggravated rather than composed by his visit. Above all, he had failed to secure American official recognition for the Republic and that, added to the closed doors at Versailles, ended whatever slim hopes there had been that Britain would agree to full Irish sovereignty.

The raids by Volunteers for arms and ammunition had given way, in the first months of 1920, to a more aggressive phase in the independence struggle when raids and arrests by crown forces were answered by Volunteer attacks on barracks. Curfew was imposed in various towns and this facilitated night raiding by police and military. Markets and fairs in proclaimed districts were suppressed, gravely affecting the day-to-day economic life of parts of the countryside. In the early hours of 20 March 1920, Tomás MacCurtain was shot dead at his home in Cork in the presence of his wife and family by a group of men with blackened faces. A characteristic figure of the cultural-nationalist ferment of the time, MacCurtain was commandant of the Cork Brigade of the IRA and had only a short time before been unanimously elected Lord Mayor of Cork. The coroner's jury returned a verdict that he had been 'wilfully murdered under circumstances of most callous brutality; that the murder was organised and carried out by the Royal Irish Constabulary, officially directed by the British Government'.

About this time Sir Nevil Macready was given control

of the military forces in Ireland. According to the *Morning Post* newspaper, he had been instructed 'to suppress the rebellion by whatever means may be requisite'. Two new categories of forces were now introduced into Ireland – the 'Black-and-Tans' (thus popularly dubbed because of their attire of khaki coats and black trousers and caps, the nickname being borrowed from a celebrated Co. Tipperary hunt pack), workless ex-soldiers who were to be paid ten shillings a day; and the Auxiliaries ('Auxies'), young ex-army officers freed from the usual restrictions of military discipline and paid at the rate of one pound a day. Both were officially classed as police auxiliaries in accordance with the British government's wish to depict the Irish 'troubles' as essentially a domestic or civil disturbance and not as a rebellion involving military operations.

One of the most remarkable and successful aspects of passive resistance was the use of the weapon of hunger-strike by Republican prisoners. The most widely publicised of these strikes was that undertaken by Terence MacSwiney who, on succeeding Tomás MacCurtain as Lord Mayor of Cork, had expressed the prophetic opinion that 'it is not those who can inflict the most but those who can suffer the most who will conquer'. As well as representing Mid-Cork in Dáil Éireann, MacSwiney commanded the First Cork Brigade of the IRA. He was also a writer and dramatist, a figure moulded to a great extent by the Gaelic League. He was arrested in August 1920 and courtmartialled on a charge of possessing seditious documents. Refusing to recognise the court, he declared that as a protest against his arrest he would refuse food while in jail. The progress of his hunger-strike in Brixton prison was followed with intense interest at home and received wide publicity abroad. His death on 25 October 1920, after a fast of seventy-four days, was publicly mourned throughout Ireland.

While hunger-strikes were a moral triumph for the Sinn Féin cause they belonged to a philosophy of passive resistance which, unfortunately perhaps, increasingly gave ground to a much more violent policy. From the spring-summer of 1920 there developed that guerilla warfare which some would see as an early example of twentieth-century wars of liberation. If it be true that terrorism is the weapon of the weak against the strong then such a strategy was the only possible one to which republicans, outnumbered and ill-equipped, could resort. Using an economy of military force the IRA effectively exploited local knowledge of terrain; the fact that the Volunteers rarely wore uniform further confused the enemy. It was a ruthless conflict. Only in sentimental retrospect could the nationalist appellation of the 'four glorious years' be justified. On both sides the military forces were largely free from political or civilian control. The IRA dealt mercilessly with any of the population that gave aid, comfort or information to the Crown forces. It was a new kind of war game to which the old rules did not apply. To the English military or imperialist mind it was underhand because it was unorthodox and those who waged it were depicted as gangsters and assassins.

To what extent did nationalist Ireland support the violence and the guerillas? In 1919 there were condemnations by urban and rural district councils of Volunteer violence but these became more muted as retaliation by Crown forces increased. Support for the objectives of Sinn Féin did not necessarily mean approval of IRA actions but the excesses of the 'Tans' and the 'Auxies', as well as British intransigence in continuing to insist on a military solution, made Volunteer killings and ambushes tolerable, at least, to the nationalist population. For example, the revulsion caused by the cold-blooded IRA killing, on 21 November 1920, of 11 Englishmen who were believed to be British intelligence agents was more than balanced out when Black-and-Tans took their revenge on the same afternoon of that 'Bloody Sunday' by killing 12 people and wounding 60 at a Gaelic football match in Croke Park. There were, of course, large areas of the country in which there was relative calm and even in the embattled areas – Dublin, Cork, Limerick and the southern and western counties – many sections of the population tried to remain free of the conflict and to carry on normal activities. The sweeping success of Sinn Féin in the municipal elections of January 1920 can hardly be taken as a popular mandate for the violence especially since there had been only sporadic killings by that date.

There was much opposition from Catholic churchmen to IRA activities from 1919 to 1921. Clerical condemnations of the shootings of policemen and soldiers became perhaps less frequent from mid-1920, or at least were balanced by denunciations of British military repression. Violence, it was assumed by many of the clergy, was the work of local self-appointed groups and had not the sanction of Dáil Éireann – an assumption not without foundation. By and large, however, most Volunteers simply ignored episcopal condemnations, taking the Fenian line that ecclesiastics had no business meddling in politics.

If the attitude of the population at large was rather ambivalent, there was little doubt about the sympathies of the ordinary people in the areas where ambushes and attacks on barracks were most frequent. Guerilla warfare, indeed, would have been almost impossible to conduct with any degree of success without a sympathetic population willing to provide food and shelter to small and mobile 'flying columns' and willing also to risk enemy retaliation. It is only in terms of this local support that we can explain the impressive West Cork guerilla victories of Kilmichael (28 November 1920) and Crossbarry (19 March 1921). It is true that in some instances help was forthcoming only out of fear or because of intimidation: for the most part, however, it was extended in these areas by a people steeped in the tradition of resistance to established authority. In turn, the courage and persistence of the ordinary Volunteer derived in large measure from the knowledge that his cause had popular backing. Outside the actual regions of combat the IRA had allies inside such vital areas as posts and communications, in the local authorities and among industrial and transport workers who refused to handle the enemy's warlike goods.

Though much of the guerilla struggle was conducted at local level, an important factor was the overall direction, financing and arming of the IRA. In all this, Michael Collins was indefatigable in his roles as Minister for Finance, Adjutant-General of the Volunteers and Director of Intelligence. It was this latter department, under Collins's direction, which penetrated and eventually destroyed the Dublin Castle intelligence system, an achievement beyond the resources of earlier generations of Irish revolutionaries and an essential prerequisite for success.

By the summer of 1920 the RIC had been forced to evacuate many of their smaller barracks and were withdrawing to the heavily fortified centres. On 1 May the Unionist *Irish Times* was ruefully reflecting that 'the forces of the crown are being driven back on their headquarters in Dublin by a steadily advancing enemy . . .The King's government has virtually ceased to exist south of the Boyne and west of the Shannon'. This was an alarmist view but it reflected loyalist concern that in many parts of the country British administration was breaking down. The *Daily News* (28 May 1920) believed that Sinn Féin had 'become the *de facto* government in three-quarters of Ireland'. Republican police were taking over control and carrying out the decrees of the courts set up by Dáil Éireann. These land and arbitration courts attracted widespread support particularly perhaps as they showed that they were far from being instruments of social revolution.

Britain's difficulties in administering Ireland increased after the local elections of 1920. The most novel aspect of these elections was that they were the first – apart from a celebrated experiment in Sligo a year before – to be held under a system of proportional representation, designed to give an effective voice to minorities. However, results constituted an overwhelming endorsement of Sinn Féin and gave the lie to those who claimed that the Sinn Féin victory at the 1918 General Election had been solely due to such temporary and negative factors as resentment at conscription and disillusion with parliamentarianism. The 1920 results gave Sinn Féin control of the overwhelming majority of county and rural district councils, as of the borough corporations. Tyrone and Fermanagh County Councils fell to the advanced nationalists as did twenty-three towns in the province of Ulster, the Unionists being in a majority in twenty-two. Thus, as Dorothy Macardle observes, 'the myth of a homogeneous Unionist Ulster had been exposed'. One might add that this had already been done in parliamentary elections as far back as 1885 but the effect regrettably was only to compound another myth, that of a homogeneous nationalist Ireland. At any rate, the taking of power at local level by Sinn Féin meant the widespread rejection of the British-instituted local government bodies and the acknowledgement of Dáil Éireann jurisdiction. Newly-elected Sinn Féin members of local councils increasingly found themselves the victims of harassment and arrest by Crown forces.

In military terms however, there could never be any serious question of a British defeat, despite the euphoric claims in subsequent song and story. The increase in Crown forces and the introduction of the Black-and-Tans and Auxiliaries had halted the disintegration of British rule and made an IRA victory impossible. At the time of the Truce in July 1921 it is estimated that there were fewer than 3,000 active Volunteers compared with 50,000 British military and several thousand police. The insurgents were suffering from a shortage of arms and ammunition while the morale of their supporters was beginning to crack under the strain of reprisal and the destruction of life and property. Terror and counter-terror had in fact resulted in stalemate. The growing pressure of British, American and world public opinion could not be indefinitely ignored. Increasingly, English journalists, politicians and churchmen began to clamour for a settlement. If in the face of this pressure the government persisted in embarking on a more desperate and bloody phase of its Irish campaign, it would retain the support of nobody but the Tory diehards and still be faced in the end with conceding some form of self-government. A truce, then, followed by negotiations, was only a matter of time.

There had of course already been a limited political response from the British side. But this initiative was doomed to be immediately ineffective as applied to the larger part of Ireland and in the long run a failure in the rest of the country. The coalition cabinet had long debated the provisions of the Better Government of Ireland Bill which was introduced by Lloyd George in the Commons on 22 December 1919 and given its second reading on 29 March 1920. It was conceived long before the guerilla struggle developed, and was in no sense a response to Sinn Féin demands: rather was it a modest measure of devolution, an application of the old Home Rule recipe with an admixture of partition. It is also notable that there was no nationalist presence in the Commons during its passage and that its final enactment was without benefit of any Irish voice at all. It provided for the establishment of two domestic bicameral parliaments in Ireland, one for the six north-eastern counties (Antrim, Armagh, Derry, Down, Fermanagh, Tyrone) and the other for the remaining twenty-six counties. An all-Ireland council with equal representation from North and South was to provide a common forum for the two parts of Ireland, and to the council might be transferred various functions of the two parliaments. Forty-two Irish members would continue to sit in the Westminster parliament which would retain control over defence, foreign affairs, customs and excise, navigation and trade, and imperial concerns in general. The powers delegated to the subordinate parliaments were very limited indeed. The Act further provided that if the majority of the members of either parliament had not taken the oath of allegiance to the Crown within fourteen days of the date fixed for the opening of the parliaments, then the assembly in question would be dissolved and that part of Ireland administered as a crown colony.

The Act was unacceptable to Sinn Féin: indeed, outside of Lloyd George's immediate circle there was little enthusiasm for it. But it gave the impression to American and Dominion opinion that steps were being taken to settle the Irish question. The Ulster Unionist attitude towards the Act was generally one of reluctant and negative acceptance of a *pis aller*. Sir Edward Carson had explained why he was prepared to accept a six-county unit of Unionist influence rather than the nine counties of Ulster which had been the historic area continually mentioned by Ulster loyalists ever since the first opposition to Home Rule. 'The inclusion of . . . six counties would bring under the jurisdiction of the North of Ireland Parliament 820,000 Protestants out of 890,000 in the whole province.' The six-county unit, then, was the largest territorial area compatible with comfortable Unionist control. A political entity which was founded on a crude head-count could hardly expect continuing stability.

In May 1921 elections were held under the Act to return members to the two parliaments. In the South, the republican government while rejecting the Government of Ireland Act out of hand decided to avail of the election arrangements (possibly a mistaken decision) to return members for the second Dáil Éireann. In the highly abnormal conditions prevailing (many candidates were IRA officers) it was hardly surprising that no elections were contested in the twenty-six county area and the unopposed republican deputies formed the second Dáil Éireann. The only Unionist members in the South were the four University of Dublin representatives. It was obvious in these circumstances that 'Southern Ireland' faced the grim prospect of rule as a Crown colony. But, despite plans afoot to extend the area of martial law, arrangements for a truce were already under way.

In the six counties of Northern Ireland the Unionists under Sir James Craig won 40 of the 52 seats in an election characterised by much violence. Though once again Fermanagh and Tyrone showed a nationalist majority, the Unionists were, as expected, solidly in a majority in the parliament which was opened by George V on 22 June 1921. Partition was now an established fact but a fact not yet realised by northern nationalist or southern republican. The negotiations which were soon to follow between Lloyd George and Sinn Féin could be undertaken all the more confidently on the British side in the knowledge that the

Ulster problem was out of the way for the time being at any rate.

It is clear from the coalition cabinet's minutes of 1919, from the British prime minister's manoeuvring during all that period and from the pathetically pious hope of the Council of Ireland provision that a partitioned Ireland was not an objective of British statesmanship. On the contrary, it was appreciated that partition would not only alienate even moderate nationalists but would be unwelcome to liberal American and Dominion opinion. A united Ireland would suit British policy far better, *provided* of course that such an Ireland would remain subordinate to British interests and to imperial prestige and security. Irish unity and limited self-government, 'yes'; Irish sovereignty, 'no'.

Perhaps the most spectacular action of the Anglo-Irish war – and one sanctioned by the republican government – was the burning of the Dublin Customs House by the IRA on 25 May 1921. The justification for the ruin of Gandon's masterpiece was the destruction of vital British government files. Yet behind the intransigence on both sides the moves to find avenues of negotiation continued. As far back as December 1920 Archbishop Clune of Perth had acted as a private intermediary and he was followed by others including Lord Derby, General Smuts and, perhaps most important, A. W. Cope, assistant undersecretary at Dublin Castle. It was Smuts also who largely inspired George V's conciliatory speech at the opening of the Northern Ireland parliament in Belfast, a speech which was an obvious overture to Lloyd George's offer of a conference and which prepared English opinion for an imminent settlement. In these senses it merits A. J. P. Taylor's description of 'by far the greatest service performed by a British monarch in modern times'. 'I speak from a full heart', said the King, 'when I pray that my coming to Ireland today may prove to be the first step towards an end of strife amongst her peoples, whatever their race or creed. In that hope I appeal to all Irishmen to pause, to stretch out the hand of forbearance and reconciliation, to forgive and forget and to join in making for the land which they love a new era of peace, contentment and goodwill'.

Two days afterwards, the British premier invited de Valera to a conference 'to end the ruinous conflict of centuries'. The offer, which waived any requirement about the surrender of arms, came at a time when the IRA was facing a crisis of men and ammunition and when popular morale was feeling the strain of counter-terror and reprisals. A truce was agreed to as a preliminary step to negotiations and came into effect on 11 July. It was welcomed in Ireland as a victory in itself and was hailed with relief and rejoicing. During that brilliant summer of 1921 many IRA men were the recipients of an unhealthy degree of hero-worship; their numbers became swollen by enthusiastic recruits, and the belligerent attitude of these 'trucileers' boded ill for a reasonable discussion of a future settlement.

2 Treaty and Civil War, 1921-23

Immediately on the coming into operation of the truce, de Valera conferred with Lloyd George in London. Lloyd George was not simply the devious and agile negotiator of Irish nationalist tradition: as head of a coalition government with a Unionist majority, in a no-nonsense imperialist-minded parliament, his position in his own cabinet was a weak one and, in the face of the intransigence of Sir James Craig and the Ulster Unionists, his room for manoeuvring was very limited. His offer to de Valera was considerably in advance of the meagre measure of Home Rule embodied in the Government of Ireland Act but fell far short of republican aspirations. While purporting to provide for Dominion status, it ensured that British interests would be paramount: Britain still would have naval and air rights in Ireland and would continue to recruit for her army while her products would not be subject to Irish tariffs. In addition, there must be 'full recognition of the existing powers and privileges of the parliament of Northern Ireland which cannot be abrogated except by their own consent'. De Valera on his return to Dublin submitted these terms to his cabinet and the Second Dáil, and their rejection was a foregone conclusion. Indeed, the hardening of republican attitudes within the Dáil was the mirror image of the diehard mood of the British parliament: significant straws in the wind were two decisions taken at the Dáil's session in August – the changing of de Valera's status from President of Dáil Éireann to President of the Irish Republic and, more fatefully, the taking of an oath by all deputies to 'bear true faith and allegiance' to 'the Irish Republic and the government of the Irish Republic which is Dáil Éireann'. This inflexibility overshadowed de Valera's assertion, made in the assembly about the same time, that the national aim in 1919 had been freedom and independence rather than a specific form of government 'because we are not republican doctrinaires'.

De Valera, indeed, was already putting forward as a possible solution his own notion of an independent Ireland in *external* association with the British Commonwealth. It was given expression, with perhaps deliberate vagueness, during the seemingly interminable exchanges with Lloyd George up to the end of September.

> A certain treaty of free association with the British Commonwealth group, as with a partial League of Nations, we would have been ready to recommend, and as a government to negotiate and take responsibility for, had we an assurance that the entry of the nation as a whole into such association would secure for it the allegiance of the present dissenting minority, to meet whose sentiment alone this step could be contemplated.

Such an ingenious constitutional notion was destined to be premature and could not, in the climate of the time, satisfy the interests of British prestige and security, neither could it – and this in the long run was of infinitely greater importance – ever hope to allay Ulster Protestant fears and suspicions.

De Valera tried to establish a negotiation formula which would not compromise in advance the Irish claim to independence and unity while Lloyd George was equally adamant that an Ireland outside the British Empire could not be contemplated and that Ulster could not be coerced: on the latter point, indeed, de Valera had already stated 'we do not contemplate the use of force'. Finally, the stalemate was resolved when the republican cabinet accepted Lloyd George's 'fresh invitation' of 29 September 'to a conference in London on 11 October where we can meet your delegates as spokesmen of the people whom you represent with a view to ascertaining how the association of Ireland with the community of nations known as the British Empire may best be reconciled with Irish national aspirations'. Implicit in this formula from the outset, it would reasonably seem, was some form of constitutional compromise involving the abandonment of any claim to a sovereign republic. Such a compromise was all the more inevitable since the military struggle had been a drawn one. It was de Valera's not very realistic hope, nonetheless, that a conference would agree on a treaty of association which would leave Irish sovereignty essentially unimpaired and the republic intact.

The Irish delegation to the conference, appointed by the republican cabinet and ratified by the Dáil, was led by Arthur Griffith, Minister for Foreign Affairs: the other members were Michael Collins, Minister for Finance, Robert Barton, Minister for Economic Affairs, and two Dáil members chosen for their legal knowledge, George Gavan Duffy and Éamonn Duggan. It was clear that Griffith and Collins would be by far the most important of the five, and Collins had consented only with reluctance to his own nomination. Austin Stack and Cathal Brugha, both of whom had refused to be members of the delegation, were the most intransigent republican members of the cabinet and were sure to keep a watchful, if not suspicious, eye on proceedings from Dublin. Personal animosities also presaged trouble: Collins and Brugha had been at loggerheads for some time while Erskine Childers, secretary to the delegation and a republican zealot, was regarded with hostility by Griffith. Even the confidence between de Valera and Collins was already impaired.

De Valera's decision not to participate in the negotiations can only be regarded in the light of subsequent developments as a major political blunder. His cabinet colleagues wished him to go and it was only through his own casting vote that the issue was decided. Even so, when the Dáil met to ratify the appointment of the delegates, Cosgrave proposed that de Valera should lead the delegation, pointing out that 'their best player' should not be 'among the reserves'.

The President felt, apparently, that his place was at

home to maintain national morale and to symbolise that common front of unity which he more than anyone else had created in 1917. By not entering into the negotiations he would emphasise his position as head of a sovereign state. As President, so the argument continued, he must not put himself in the position where he might be suspected of compromising on the 'Republic'. Should there be an agreement in London based on the principle of external association, his non-participation in the negotiations would make it easier for him to get intransigent republicans such as Brugha and Stack to accept what was a new and suspect concept. If, on the other hand, the negotiations should break down it was more desirable that this should happen under Griffith who had the reputation of being a moderate rather than under the President whose contacts with Lloyd George to date had stamped him in British eyes as an extremist. Above all, the delegates in London would have to refer back vital points to Dublin for decision and thus avoid the danger of snap decisions and enable them to give due deliberation to their proceedings.

It must be stressed that de Valera's absence from the delegation caused no great stir at the time but was soon revealed as a tragic mistake. Individual arguments against his attendance were surely outweighed by the imperative need for the leader of nationalist Ireland to head his delegation at such a momentous conference. Pitted against a British team which included politicians of the calibre of Lloyd George, Austen Chamberlain, Lord Birkenhead and Winston Churchill, the Irish side needed de Valera's negotiating talents. With his flair for constitutional argument, the exposition of the unfamiliar external association idea, to which de Valera attached so much importance, would best have come from the President himself. His enemies subsequently claimed that he stayed in Dublin because he wanted to avoid the odium of a compromise he knew to be inevitable. This view does him less than justice: a compromise he must have known there would have to be, but he genuinely believed that from Dublin he could regulate the degree of compromise and make it acceptable to the extremist republican element. But he placed the Irish delegates in a fatefully ambiguous position. Chosen by the cabinet and sanctioned by the Dáil, their credentials were 'as envoys plenipotentiary from the elected Government of the Republic of Ireland to negotiate and conclude on behalf of Ireland with the representatives of His Britannic Majesty George V a treaty or treaties of settlement, association and accommodation between Ireland and the community of Nations known as the British Commonwealth'. Notwithstanding these plenipotentiary powers, however, the delegates were instructed by the cabinet to notify Dublin 'before decisions are finally reached on the main questions' and to similarly submit 'the complete text of the draft treaty about to be signed'. It is clear that while the President was anxious to have the delegates regarded as plenipotentiaries of a sovereign Republic – and so secure a measure of recognition for the 'Republic' in advance – he also wanted to establish such control over the delegation as to ensure that no treaty would be signed without the prior approval of the cabinet. There was here an understandable anxiety that delegates and cabinet should be unanimous about recommending a treaty to the Dáil for acceptance or rejection but unfortunately it involved a basic confusion, not to say contradiction, between credentials and instructions which was subsequently to be the subject of much bitter dispute. This ambiguous position would not have arisen had the President been present in London.

The Irish delegation were totally inexperienced in the complex diplomatic task in which they were now to be involved for almost two months and the surprising feature is that they performed as well as they did. Faced by a brilliant team of British representatives they also had to contend with a change in the mood of the interested British public: now that a conference had actually begun and Dominion status had been offered, the onus of being 'reasonable' had shifted to the Irish side. Yet the majority of the cabinet, if not of the Dáil, had approached these negotiations without facing up to the hard realities. Even if the British government – itself a coalition – had been willing to concede full separation, it was far too dependent on Tory support in the Commons and in the country to have done so. Again, the idea of external association was simply not adequate to satisfy the demands of British security or propitiate British self-esteem. It was, moreover, doubtful if after such a long truce the IRA was in any condition to renew hostilities or the people to endure them. Above all, what should not have been overlooked was the newly established constitutional security of Northern Ireland and the determination of its Unionist leaders to hold on to what they had. However, to the uncompromising republican elements in the cabinet and the Dáil these practical considerations were irrelevant: for them the republic one and indivisible already existed with a compelling mystique of its own. To attempt to disestablish it would be treason and a violation of the oath they had sworn to uphold it.

There were three main points at issue in the Treaty negotiations: What was to be the constitutional status of a new Irish state? What was to be the position of north-east Ulster? What provisions were to be made for British defence and security? More easily resolvable were the questions of financial and trade relations. The discussions between the two sides took place at first in full conference and later in smaller groups. Here Collins and Griffith came to be the really important men on the Irish side and their Irish enemies afterwards alleged that this was a deliberate isolation strategy on the part of Lloyd George. In reality it was the most convenient method of carrying on complex negotiations: the British delegation had other government business to attend to and, as well, continuous full-scale conferences were highly impracticable.

From the British standpoint the key problem was to secure Irish allegiance to the Crown and acceptance of Dominion status. Lloyd George could not secure support in the Commons for any greater concession: had the prime minister dared to do battle on the issue the result would simply have been the replacement of his coalition government by an intransigent Unionist one. Over-generous concessions to the Irish would mean a dangerous boost to independence movements in India and elsewhere in the Empire. Acceptance of the Crown was vital to British prestige and security, yet the symbol of the Crown was obnoxious to Irish republicans, though hardly to the nationalist population at large. As for Dominion status, its potentialities for evolution to full sovereignty were not at all apparent in 1921. The dominions were developing towards equality in practice, but in law and in constitutional form they still occupied a subordinate position with respect to the United Kingdom. There were very real restrictions on their freedom in the sphere of foreign policy. When the British negotiators pointed to Canada as an example of the freedom of the Dominions in practice, the Irish delegates could reasonably reply that Canada with her physical vastness and her geographical remoteness from the mother-country could make light of constitutional limitations whereas Ireland as a dominion would be vulnerably small and close. Dominion status, it could be argued moreover, was natural for former colonies such as Australia and Canada but should not be forced on an ancient nation like Ireland.

It is rather surprising that the Irish should have been prepared to meet British requirements on defence without any great fuss, though it is debatable whether Irish independence, or future Irish neutrality, could be at all reconciled with the presence of British naval bases. At any rate, this was never a major bone of contention either during the negotiations or afterwards in the Dáil debates on the Treaty. But the two main problems, constitutional status and national unity, seemed to be intractable. Griffith put forward the external association scheme at a plenary session on 24 October. 'On the one hand Ireland will consent to adhere for all purposes of common agreed concern to the League of Sovereign States associated and known as the British Commonwealth of Nations. On the other hand Ireland calls upon Great Britain to renounce all claims and authority over Ireland and Irish affairs'. Lloyd George wanted to move the Irish delegates from this (to British minds) incomprehensible position and was confident that he could get them to accept the Crown more directly if he could satisfy them that Ireland's 'essential unity' would not be lost: indeed, it was the Irish delegation's initial strategy to make this latter issue the breaking point of the negotiations. And this showed a proper sense of values: had not nationalist Ireland turned to Sinn Féin, after all, in part at least because the Irish Party had become tarred with the brush of partition? Yet the crux now was that Craig and the Ulster Unionists already established in Northern Ireland had no intention of vacating possession, or of putting an Ulster parliament under Dublin sovereignty. In the face of Ulster adamance, Lloyd George brought up the idea of a Boundary Commission which would, or so the delegates were encouraged to believe, delimit the six-county area, award Tyrone, Fermanagh and other northern nationalist areas to the South and so make the ultimate survival of Northern Ireland impossible. Gradually this idea began to be accepted by Griffith and Collins at least as a practical alternative to immediate all-Ireland unity.

After a weekend in Dublin in late November, the Irish delegates presented in London on 28 November a memorandum which had the approval of their cabinet. While Irish legislative and executive authority were to be regarded as deriving exclusively from the elected representatives of the people, nevertheless 'Ireland shall agree to be associated with the British Commonwealth for purposes of common concern such as defence, peace and war; and she shall recognise the British Crown as head of the association; and that, as a token of that recognition, she shall vote an annual sum to the King's Civil List'. But *recognition* was not the same as *allegiance*. When after further days of argument at the negotiating table the delegates once more returned to Dublin on 2 December for what was to be the final consultation with the cabinet, Griffith, Collins and Duggan stated their conviction that Lloyd George would not budge on the question of an oath of allegiance to the Crown and that he would not tolerate the exclusion of the Crown from purely Irish affairs. Barton and Gavan Duffy, however, believed that the British premier was still employing a considerable amount of bluff. The cabinet meeting was marked by tension and bitterness particularly after Brugha had made the offensive statement that in dealing particularly with Griffith and Collins, 'the British government selected its men'. Eventually something like agreement was restored when Griffith appears to have promised not to sign any document involving allegiance to the Crown or inclusion within the Empire. Yet the plenipotentiaries returned to London in a state of uncertainty.

Lloyd George now expressed anger at the Irish reluctance to come to a final agreement. To Collins he emphasised that after the Boundary Commission had re-drawn the frontier with Northern Ireland, economic realities would ensure Irish unity. When Griffith tried to press Lloyd George to get Craig to agree to Irish unity before the form of Irish association with the Empire should be finalised, the British premier dramatically produced a note which Griffith had assented to on 13 November at a time when Lloyd George had said he needed reassurances to placate Tory diehard opinion and in which Griffith had agreed to the Boundary Commission idea as at least a temporary solution of the Ulster difficulty. The production of the note at this stage compelled Griffith to declare he would stand by his word. The opportunity to 'break on Ulster' was finally gone. There were increased concessions in respect of fiscal autonomy, trade and defence. After Lloyd George had modified the oath of allegiance to make it more palatable to the Irish delegation, Griffith was prepared to sign an agreement. The wily Welshman now presented his theatrical ultimatum. The Irish delegates must sign an agreement *now* 'or else quit': he would send one of two letters in his hand to Craig that night – one contained news of a settlement, the other of a final breakdown. 'If I send this letter, it is war, and war within three days. Which letter am I to send?' Collins, then Duggan, and after several hours Barton and Gavan Duffy, decided to accept the agreement. In the early hours of 6 December 1921 both sides signed the 'Articles of agreement for a treaty between Great Britain and Ireland'.

The Irish Free State was to have the same constitutional status in the British Empire as Canada, Australia, New Zealand and South Africa. In fact, Canada – the most important of the Dominions – was to serve as the model of Ireland's relations with the Imperial Parliament and Government. The Crown's representative in Ireland was to be appointed in the same way as the governor-general of Canada. The oath to be taken by members of the Parliament of the Irish Free State was not, however, to be a simple oath of loyalty to the King as in the other Dominions: it was to be primarily an oath of allegiance to the 'constitution of the Irish Free State' and only secondarily would members swear to be faithful to 'King George V, his heirs and successors by law in virtue of the common citizenship of Ireland with Great Britain and her adherence to and membership of the group of nations forming the British Commonwealth of Nations'. The Irish Free State was to afford specific naval facilities in time of peace to Great Britain with an extension of these facilities in time of war. Thus at Berehaven, Queenstown, Belfast Lough and Lough Swilly the harbour defences were 'to remain in charge of British care and maintenance parties'. The articles of agreement further provided that no law should be made in Ireland establishing a state religion or discriminating between citizens on religious grounds. Another article laid down that as an interim measure 'steps shall be taken forthwith for summoning a meeting of members of Parliament elected for constituencies in Southern Ireland since the passing of the Government of Ireland Act 1920, and for constituting a provisional government' to which the British authorities would transfer the necessary powers and machinery.

There were provisions for dealing with the Irish Free State's liability for servicing the public debt and with the question of paying equable compensation to public servants who would retire or who would be dismissed by reason of the change of government. But perhaps the most important sections of what was to be commonly referred to as 'the Treaty' were those relating to Northern Ireland. The phraseology of the document in general seemed to visualise Ireland as a unit but Article XII provided for Northern Ireland's right to reject the jurisdiction of the Irish Free State, and for the provisions of the Government of Ireland Act 1920 'including those relating to the Council of Ireland' to continue to apply to Northern Ireland. In this case, the article continued, 'a commission consisting of three persons, one to be appointed by the government of the Irish Free State, one to be appointed by the government of Northern Ireland and one who shall be chairman to be appointed by the British government shall determine in accordance with the wishes of the inhabitants, so far as may be compatible with economic and geographic conditions, the boundaries between Northern Ireland and the rest of Ireland . . .'

In his *Peace by Ordeal,* Lord Longford's assessment of the Treaty is 'a political bargain which was practically mean but generous in the context of centuries of misrule and generous coming from men in whose bones the very marrow was steeped in colonialism'. From an Irish nationalist viewpoint the constitutional provisions not only represented a spectacular advance on the modest devolution proposals of 1912, 1916 and 1920 but were a substantial improvement on Lloyd George's offer of July 1921. It must be remembered that the proposal of Dominion status first put forward by Asquith in 1919 had at that time been denounced by Lloyd George as insane and that it was still anathema to many English imperialists who feared the evolutionary development of the Dominions. The evidence available since then to historians confirms that the final proposals on constitutional status put forward by the British delegation represented the limit to which any British government could at that time go. It is not only the hindsight of the historian but the foresight of Collins and Griffith which prompts the now commonplace reflection that the Treaty contained all the seeds of future constitutional fulfilment. Besides, Dominion status and the Crown were essential prerequisites for any possible reconciliation with the northern Unionists. Sovereignty and unity were irreconcilable concepts and more could have been made of this point subsequently by the pro-Treatyites.

In many areas, admittedly minor ones, the Treaty was a victory for Sinn Féin: the Irish Free State was to have full governmental control over finance, customs, tariffs and economic policy as well as over the judiciary, the police and the army. The least satisfactory aspect was the section dealing with Northern Ireland. Here the Irish delegation had failed disastrously to make a 'break on Ulster', a point where they might have counted on a good deal of British support and sympathy. They were outmanoeuvred by the devious tactics of Lloyd George but even more badly served by the constitutional obsessions of de Valera and the republican extremists. The will-o'-the-wisp of sovereignty had been pursued at the expense of unity and in the end neither was served. Whether a more prudent policy would have avoided partition, given the intractability of the Ulster question, remains problematic. But there is little doubt that the Irish delegation was lured into accepting a vague boundary commission proposal without demanding international adjudication or clearer terms of reference. Yet ironically it was not primarily for their failure to secure national unity that the delegates were to be so vehemently repudiated by a large minority of their fellow-countrymen.

The republican cabinet split on the issue at once, Brugha and Stack being at one with de Valera in rejecting the Treaty while W. T. Cosgrave supported Griffith, Collins and Barton. De Valera publicly revealed the dissension in the cabinet but stated 'there is a definite constitutional way of resolving our political differences'. The cabinet split prefigured a tragic division in the Dáil and more ominously in the Army. As the common front which was Sinn Féin began to break under the crisis, hitherto half-hidden personal antagonisms came into the open. The harsh mutual recriminations, the accusations of treachery and the increasingly venomous tone which were to characterise the Treaty debates cannot be explained solely in terms of disagreement, albeit profound, over principles. (

38

Though de Valera claimed that 'the terms of the agreement are in violent conflict with the wishes of the majority of the nation' all the evidence is that initial popular reaction to the Treaty was favourable. There was general relief that a settlement had been reached and appreciation that the substance of independence seemed to have been secured. This was certainly the impression to be gathered from the sentiments expressed by local bodies, the county council of de Valera's Clare stronghold, for example, coming out in favour of the Treaty. Yet it was the nationally elected representatives of the people who were to decide the great issue in a marathon discussion and in an atmosphere of drama, indeed at times of theatricality.

The Dáil met on 14 December 1921 to commence discussion on ratification or rejection of the Treaty. (The British parliament was to ratify the agreement on 16 December by substantial majorities in both houses.) When the plenipotentiaries were accused of not having submitted the final text to Dublin, Collins and Griffith replied that their signatures had not committed the Dáil whose responsibility it now was to reject or approve the Treaty. De Valera put forward his own alternative to the Treaty. This was to become known as Document No. 2 and it enshrined his favourite idea of external association while cmitting the oath and the provision for a governor-general. But it was vain to hope that the British would accept such a proposal; a treaty had been signed, and in any case external association had already been rejected and Ireland's inclusion in the Empire insisted on. De Valera's proposal failed to gain the united support of the Dáil and he withdrew it from public discussion for the moment. Document No. 2, be it noted, had no new proposals on the partition question.

It was Griffith who introduced the motion that the Dáil should approve the Treaty. He claimed it meant the end of seven centuries of British occupation and that the oath was one 'that any Irishman could take with honour'. He cited Thomas Davis (one of the formative influences on his thinking): 'Peace with England, alliance with England to some extent and, under certain circumstances, confederation with England; but an Irish ambition, Irish hopes, strength, virtue and rewards for the Irish'. There was, said Griffith, no real alternative to the Treaty except a quibble: the choice, in fact, was 'between half recognising the British king and the British empire and marching in . . . with our heads up'. In any case, he said sensibly as well as prophetically, the Treaty 'has no more finality than that we are the final generation on the face of the earth'. After Scán MacEoin, the redoubtable guerilla leader, had supported Griffith, de Valera asked the Dáil not to approve the Treaty saying it did not satisfy Irish national aspirations and that they in the Dáil had been elected 'to be the guardians of an independent Irish state' and could not vote away that independence. Collins argued that the very acceptance of an invitation to a conference in itself constituted a compromise and that by agreeing to negotiations de Valera had thereby acknowledged that a republic was out of the question. Collins asserted, in a memorable phrase, that the Treaty 'gives us freedom, not the ultimate freedom that all nations desire and develop to, but the freedom to achieve it'. Erskine Childers, who had been secretary to the delegation, admitted there had been no question of securing an isolated republic but claimed that the plenipotentiaries had failed to bring about an acceptable and honourable association with England. Ireland's position under the Treaty would depend on an act of the British parliament: Ireland under the Treaty would be 'virtually a protectorate of England'. Kevin O'Higgins admitted that there had been compulsion in the final phase of the treaty negotiations but was nevertheless positively in favour of Commonwealth membership. He expressed his belief, in a prescient phrase, in 'the evolution of this group . . . towards a condition, not merely of individual freedom but also of equality of status'.

With some exceptions, the rest of the debate was tedious, repetitive and increasingly bitter. Treaty supporters claimed that no better terms could be arranged, that war was the alternative, that the choice posed by their opponents was not between the Treaty and a sovereign republic but between the Treaty and Document No. 2. which was in any case unacceptable to Britain. Many opponents of the Treaty flatly stated they could not accept dominion status and an oath of allegiance: they had sworn an oath to the republic and therefore could not vote for the Treaty. The ghosts of the republican martyrs – 'MacDonagh's bony thumb', in Yeats's phrase – hovered over many of the anti-Treaty speakers and especially over the small but formidable regiment of women deputies all six of whom vigorously opposed the agreement. They included Miss Mary MacSwiney, sister of the already legendary Lord Mayor of Cork, and Mrs Tom Clarke, widow of one of the executed signatories to the 1916 Proclamation.

The Dáil adjourned on 22 December for Christmas and the recess helped substantially to swing support for the Treaty. Deputies who hitherto were opposed to the agreement were lobbied by their constituents or pressured by pulpit and press and returned to the resumed debate with their minds made up to support the Treaty.

When the Dáil reconvened on 3 January 1922, Collins suggested that the opponents of the Treaty might abstain from voting in a division and that they should 'allow the Treaty to go through and let the Provisional Government come into existence; and if necessary you can fight the Provisional Government on the Republic question afterwards'. In the event the proposal was unacceptable as were other attempts at mediation. On 6 January, the second last day of the debate, de Valera recalled, in the course of a long speech, that for four years he had held the balance between the antagonistic viewpoints which Griffith and Brugha represented and that he had succeeded until the Treaty was signed. Document No. 2 was a policy which he felt the Irish people wanted. Another famous phrase of his emerged from the debates: 'whenever I wanted to know what the Irish people wanted I had only to examine my own heart and it told me straight off what the Irish people wanted'. A little later, the man who was to dominate the Irish scene for the next generation expressed himself as being 'sick and tired of politics—so sick that no matter what happens I would go back to private life'!

On 7 January, the final day of the long debate, Brugha made a personal attack on Collins who, he said, had been the object of an unwarranted personality cult. He suggested that the plenipotentiaries should now refrain from voting on the issue, but Griffith in his closing speech refused, as he said, to 'dishonour my signature'. He claimed he and the other plenipotentiaries had been sent to London to make a compromise or bargain and this they had done. Referring to Document No. 2 he said he did not believe that 'the people of Ireland should be sacrificed for a formula'.

The vote was at last taken: there were 64 votes for the Treaty and 57 against. Collins then pleaded for some kind of unity at least during the transition period from British to Irish government but Mary MacSwiney stated that approval of the Treaty was a gross act of betrayal and there could be no co-operation between the representatives of the Irish republic 'and the so-called Free State'. De Valera's final emotional word was on the 'magnificent discipline' of the previous four years. As he broke down, unable to continue, Brugha promised that discipline would be maintained in the army. The long, dramatic debate was at an end: the confusion and division were only beginning.

Only an insignificant amount of the Dáil's Treaty debates related to Ulster. (The most fearfully real questions for deputies were the nature of dominion status, the acceptability of the oath of allegiance, the position of the Crown, and the abandonment of the almost mystical republic.) Although Sinn Féin had triumphed over the parliamentarians in part at least, because the latter seemed willing to accept a compromise on national unity, it inherited much of the complacency, indeed ignorance, which nationalist Ireland had long exhibited towards Northern Protestants. Like the Irish Party, Sinn Féin underestimated the tenacity and passion of Ulster Unionism. It tended to assume that once the Northern Protestant really understood the Sinn Féin philosophy—and experienced British government pressures—his resistance to a united Ireland would disappear. It paid lip service to the ideal of Irish brotherhood yet was grossly insensitive to Ulster fears and susceptibilities. By sanctioning a boycott of Belfast merchants, the Dáil allowed itself to make the colossal blunder of treating one section of the country as alien while professing itself to be an all-Ireland assembly. Indeed its view of itself as an all-Ireland body rested on self-deception: some deputies, it is true, represented Northern Ireland constituencies but in all cases except one they also sat for southern constituencies which were their real interest base, so to speak. Dáil Éireann was in practice the assembly of a virtually homogeneous nationalist Ireland and its attitude to the north-east, as demonstrated in those years and for many a decade thereafter, was characterised more by a concern for territorial unity rather than by any real desire to achieve a brotherhood of all Irishmen.

Even when Collins looked to the Treaty as providing the means for North-South reconciliation, he seemed to be sharing the complacent and naive nationalist assumption that the Ulster Unionist would readily respond to the correct mixture of southern overtures and firm British pressure. Collins's apparent hope that the Boundary Commission would effect significant territorial changes and thus end partition by erosion, as it were, suggests another plausible reason for the non-appearance of the Ulster issue in the Treaty debates. It appears that both friend and foe shared Collins's hope, based on the verbal assurances of Birkenhead and Churchill, that the Commission could reduce Northern Ireland to a four-county area which would soon disappear either through its own economic non-viability or through British pressure or both. It mattered not, apparently, that the relevant clause in the Treaty did not bear this optimistic interpretation: nor did anyone advert to the possibility that, even if the Commission succeeded in delimiting the territory of Northern Ireland, the reduced area might not conveniently wither away but might rather take firmer root in the more favourable soil of a greater cultural, economic and political homogeneity.

What were the practical effects of the Dáil ratification of the Treaty? Not, as one might expect, the immediate disestablishment of the Republic and the direct setting up of the temporary political machinery which would institute the Irish Free State. On 9 January 1922 de Valera announced that he and his cabinet were resigning. Mrs Clarke, supported by Liam Mellowes, proposed that he be re-elected President of the Irish Republic but the motion was rejected by the very slim majority of 60 votes to 58, a result which in the circumstances was a tribute to de Valera's personal stature. Griffith paid a generous tribute to the defeated president who in reply hoped that nobody would 'talk of fratricidal strife. That is all nonsense'. The opponents of the Treaty would not interfere with the other side 'except when we find that you are going to do something that will definitely injure the Irish nation'.

Collins, seconded by General Richard Mulcahy, now proposed that Griffith should form an executive. His anti-Treaty opponents warned that Griffith could not form a Provisional Government from the Dáil which was the parliament of the Republic but rather that he should convene the 'Parliament of Southern Ireland' and form his provisional government from that body. Griffith promised that he would fill the same position as his predecessor, de Valera, and that he would 'keep the Republic in being until such time as the establishment of the Free State is put to the people to decide for or against'. When the election of Griffith as president of the Dáil was moved, de Valera led his supporters from the House amidst a barrage of abusive exchanges and Griffith was elected President. His ministers included Collins (Finance), Mulcahy (Defence), Gavan Duffy, Duggan, Cosgrave and O'Higgins.

When de Valera and his followers returned, the Dáil had to switch its attention from politics and constitutional dissensions to hear a deputation of the Irish Labour Party led by Thomas Johnson who warned his hearers of the necessity to organise the resources of the country for the betterment of the common people. His estimate of the critical unemployment situation was that there were 130,000 people out of work. The deputation reminded the deputies, but only fleetingly, that there were pressing social and economic issues to be dealt with and that organised labour, though it had stood aside up to now, would be an active political force in the new state.

Before the Dáil adjourned for over a month de Valera asserted that the new 'President of the Republic will receive from me personally, and I hope from every citizen while he is acting in that capacity, the fullest respect which his office entitles him to'. At the same time de Valera warned that he would do everything in his power 'to see this established Republic is not disestablished'. Finally, Richard Mulcahy gave his assurance that 'the army will remain the army of the Irish Republic'.

In accordance with Article 17 of the Treaty, the 'Parliament of Southern Ireland' assembled on 14 January 1922. It had been convened by Griffith acting in his capacity as 'chairman of the Irish delegation of Plenipotentiaries'. The summons was sent to the elected representatives of the twenty-six county area. It was ignored by the anti-Treaty deputies and the attendance comprised sixty pro-Treaty members of Dáil Éireann as well as the four members for Dublin University. The parliament approved of the Treaty, elected a provisional government under Collins's chairmanship and then dissolved. Cosgrave, Duggan, O'Higgins, P. J. Hogan (Agriculture) and Joseph McGrath (Labour) were ministers of Dáil Éireann: they were now also ministers of the provisional government which in addition included Fionán Lynch and Eoin MacNeill. The dual ministerial role was only one of the ambiguities and anomalies which now prevailed.

On 16 January the provisional government went to Dublin Castle, the seat of British rule in Ireland for centuries, and a formal transfer of power took place. Evacuation of British troops from the twenty-six county area began and the notorious Auxiliaries and Black-and-Tans as well as the Royal Irish Constabulary began to be disbanded. Recruiting for a new paid, uniformed and un-armed police force – the *Garda Síochána* or Civic Guards – took place. Some of these were drawn from the voluntary republican police which had served the Sinn Féin regime over the previous two or three years: however, those known to be antagonistic to the Treaty were not invited to join.

Meanwhile, Collins was intent on making the Treaty work and threw himself into the complex task of taking over the machinery of government from the British authorities. He had to travel several times to London to confer with Churchill at the Colonial Office. There was the darkening cloud of the growing division in the South as well as the prospect of further trouble in the North. Craig and the Northern Protestants were determined to maintain the territorial integrity of the Northern state. Even should the Boundary Commission realise all of Collins's expectations, the nationalist minority was ex-posed in the interim to the attacks of Protestants, angered by the Boundary Commission clause. If the 1920 pogrom which had provoked the retaliatory boycott were repeated there could well be intervention from republicans in the South. This was the background to the Collins-Craig agreement in London on 21 January whereby Collins undertook to lift the Belfast boycott in return for Craig's promise to prevent attacks on Northern Catholics and to protect Catholic shipyard workers. But trouble continued in the border areas and the government in Belfast brought in stringent measures under the Special Powers Act to deal with illegal activity. Rioting and arson flared as the recently-created A- and B-special constabulary forces championed the Protestants while both pro- and anti-Treaty IRA supported the Catholic minority who were now beginning to realise in despair that the Border promised to be more than a temporary arrangement. The Protestants for their part felt a threat to their position from the growing intransigence of the anti-Treaty forces in the South. Belfast bore the brunt of the internecine strife. Ninety-eight of the 138 casualties there in February were

Catholic and there were 33 killings in one night. The death toll continued with 60 people killed in Belfast in March, and an ominous development was Craig's appointment of the rabidly anti-nationalist Sir Henry Wilson as his adviser on law and order. Another North-South agreement in March failed to stop the sectarian strife: by June, 93 Protestants and 171 Catholics had been killed in the months since the signing of the Treaty and refugees had fled in their thousands from the troubled province. Despite his acceptance of the Treaty, his position as chairman of the provisional government and his close liaison with the British authorities, Collins could not ignore the plight of the Northern nationalists. Indeed, while on the verge of war with his former comrades in the South, he found himself in the anomalous position of sanctioning the supply of arms to the IRA in the North irrespective of what position they took on the Treaty issue.

An armed conflict in the South was not an inevitable consequence of the Treaty split and the confused period from January to June 1922 was marked by several attempts to head off fratricidal strife. There is little doubt that the Treaty commanded majority support: this was to be made plain in both the 1922 and 1923 elections. It was favoured in the first place by all those who sought a quick return to peace and order. Those whose livelihood depended on trade were quick to support the Treaty as were church leaders of all denominations, though a handful of Catholic clergymen remained republican in sympathy. A joint pastoral from the Catholic hierarchy was to condemn the anti-Treatyites unequivocally later in 1922. The Treaty was also welcomed by most of the press, by former Home Rulers and by the southern Unionists. These latter had reconciled themselves rather rapidly to the shape of things to come and so guaranteed that they would be tolerated, at least, in the new order. Supporters of the Treaty also included those who were attracted by the prospect of army or civil service careers in the new state. Then there were the politically involved who, like Collins himself, believed the Treaty was a stepping stone to full independence, that partition would not last and that the British Empire was in decline. Many lesser figures were content to take their cue from Collins.

The considerable influence of the IRB was also thrown behind the Treaty. As president of the Brotherhood, Collins was in a key position to shape the attitude of the organisation. As early as 10 December 1921, the Supreme Council had decided, despite the protests of a few like Liam Lynch, that the Treaty should be approved: however, those members who were public representatives were to be free to decide for themselves. At first sight it seems anomalous that a body with a separatist philosophy should have taken such a stand but there was also a tradition of pragmatism in the Brotherhood and it clearly shared the view of Collins that the Treaty offered the freedom to achieve freedom. Whether the IRB attitude made a vital difference to Treaty support remains a matter of debate.

Against the Treaty were those who were willing to follow any lead which de Valera gave. Cumann na mBan, now more militant than ever, imitated the example of the women Dáil deputies. Parts of Ireland where there was a long tradition of political or social resistance and, more particularly, where the Anglo-Irish struggle had been intense, were in no mood for compromise: this was true of some southern areas where there were such influential military leaders as Liam Lynch and Tom Barry. There were also those for whom the prospect of a return to humdrum life held little attraction and there were the 'trucileers' with their new-found enthusiasm for the Republic. But to many republicans the Treaty was unacceptable simply because it betrayed the Republic and the martyred dead and, to a lesser extent, because it was associated with partition. For a socialist minority, the Treaty was a betrayal on another level: it was a blow to the prospect of establishing the Workers' Republic.

The most ominous aspect of the split was the sharp division on the Treaty in the volunteer army of the Republic, both at headquarters staff and throughout the country at large. The attitude of any given group of

Volunteers was frequently determined by the position taken by its commanding officer. The majority of headquarters staff, including Collins and Mulcahy, were pro-Treaty though they were opposed by such formidable military leaders as Liam Mellowes and Rory O'Connor. Throughout the country a majority of divisional commandants, including Oscar Traynor and Liam Lynch, were adamant in their opposition to the Treaty. Lynch put his position very simply: 'we have declared for an Irish Republic and will not live under any other law'. The tradition of army independence of civilian control, dating back to the regrouping of the Volunteers in 1917, now appeared in an ominous light. The anti-Treaty officers deplored the Dáil's sanction of the Treaty and, despite Mulcahy's assurances, feared the army might be used to 'disestablish the Republic'. On 11 January 1922 these officers requested of Mulcahy that a general army convention be held which would renew the army's allegiance to the Republic and place it under the supreme control of an executive appointed by the convention—in other words, a return to independent military control. Such a convention assembled on 26 March, despite the Dáil cabinet's prohibition, and it consisted of anti-Treaty men only. It appointed an executive which was to be the army's supreme authority. This executive repudiated the authority of the Dáil Minister for Defence and demanded that recruitment for the provisional government army force and for the Civic Guards should cease. The pro-Treatyites regarded the executive as an attempt to set up a military dictatorship. Meanwhile various sections of the army were hardening into definite pro- or anti-Treaty units: where barracks were being taken over from the evacuating British military, the replacing garrison was in some places pro-, and in others anti-Treaty. The rival factions sometimes confronted each other and were involved in as yet minor clashes. The officers and men who declared for acceptance of the Treaty were armed and uniformed by the Provisional Government and these became the nucleus of the 'national' or future Free State Army. This development was regarded by the

ELAINE

anti-Treatyites, or the 'Irregulars', as they came to be called, as a breach of Mulcahy's undertaking that the IRA would be maintained as the Army of the Republic. Thus the first rumblings of a military struggle grew louder.

On the political side, Sinn Féin held its annual Ard-Fheis on 21 February. The delegates, the majority of whom were anti-Treaty, were concerned to avoid a break in the historic movement and were glad to accept a proposal drafted by de Valera and Griffith which stipulated that the Ard-Fheis would stand adjourned and elections be postponed for at least three months so that the people would have an opportunity to consider the texts both of the Treaty and of the new constitution. Thus a precarious unity was for the moment preserved.

In March de Valera constituted the main body of the deputies who had supported him in the Treaty vote into what looked like a political organisation—*Cumann na Poblachta*. His attitudes in these months seemed ambiguous, if not vacillating. For him 'the dilemma of the Treaty' was 'the conflict between two principles, majority rule on the one hand and the inalienability of the national sovereignty on the other'. A number of speeches which de Valera made in March sounded extremely sanguinary, though he and his subsequent apologists maintained that they were simply intended to be dire warnings of the grim consequences that would follow acceptance of the Treaty. The best-known of these speeches was made at Thurles just after the prohibition of the Volunteer convention had become known:

> If they accepted the Treaty and if the Volunteers of the future tried to complete the work the Volunteers of the last four years had been attempting, they would have to complete it, not over the bodies of foreign soldiers, but over the dead bodies of their own countrymen. They would have to wade through Irish blood, through the blood of the soldiers of the Irish government and through, perhaps, the blood of some of the members of the Government in order to get Irish freedom.

But the anti-Treaty army officers made their fateful decisions in complete independence of de Valera. On 14 April some of them occupied the Four Courts and set up their headquarters there. This was a blatant challenge to the authority of the provisional government, yet it was a challenge which Collins was unwilling to take up not only because he desperately sought every means to avoid war with old comrades but because a precipitate move against the Four Courts garrison might spark off a conflict. It was understandable that he and Mulcahy should have been anxious to avoid confrontation whereas Griffith and O'Higgins had the essentially civilian viewpoint that the army must be firmly brought under government control. This crisis came at a time when the provisional government was trying to achieve the almost impossible task of hammering out a constitution which would be acceptable at once to de Valera's side and to the watchful British government.

When at the end of April a meeting of de Valera, Brugha, Collins, Griffith and various intermediaries could not agree on how to 'secure a peaceful election', another attempt at restoring unity was made by army officers from both sides. On 1 May, the 'Army Document', drafted by leading officers from both sides, pleaded for army unification 'on the basis of the acceptance and utilisation of our present national position in the best interests of Ireland'. It recommended 'the acceptance of the fact—admitted by all sides—that the majority of the people of Ireland are willing to accept the Treaty' and 'an agreed election with a view to forming a government which will have the confidence of the whole country'. Though Rory O'Connor rejected the Army Document, it made further negotiations possible. The great political problem was to secure agreement on whether and how to make the Treaty an election issue, since the anti-Treatyites had good reason to fear an adverse popular verdict.

The final peace-making attempt was the famous Collins-de Valera pact of 20 May, agreed to by the Dáil and the provisional government despite Griffith's obvious reluctance. A national coalition panel of candidates representing the two sides in Sinn Féin was to be put forward for the third Dáil. The number allowed to each side was to be in proportion to its existing strength in the Dáil. All would stand in the name of Sinn Féin. As well, 'every and any interest is free to go up and contest the election equally with the National Sinn Féin panel'. After the election, a coalition government would comprise an elected president, the minister for defence representing the army and nine other ministers, five to be chosen by the majority party and four by the minority. The reason for the arrangement was declared to be that 'the national position requires the entrusting of the government of the country into the joint hands of those who have been the strength of the national situation during the last few years without prejudice to their present respective positions'. By any measurement, this extraordinary document was a triumph for the opponents of the Treaty, since it would prevent a direct expression of the people's views on the issue. It was condemned by the British since, if fully implemented, it would return a government with four republicans opposed to the Treaty. The British were also determined that the draft constitution which the provisional government was trying to make as acceptable as possible to the republicans must be kept strictly in accordance with the provisions of the Treaty.

As election day approached against a growing background of bomb explosions, snipings and other incidents, Collins came to the conclusion that the pact would not work within a constitution which had been amended to meet British objections and which the provisional government now accepted. Accordingly, speaking at Cork at a pre-election rally, Collins effectively repudiated the pact, saying he was 'not hampered now by being on a platform where there are coalitionists'. The republicans subsequently made much of the repudiation as they did of the fact that the draft constitution became available to the electorate in the newspapers only on the morning of the election, 16 June. The constitution set the Irish Free State firmly within the framework of the British Empire. The legislature was to consist of the King and two houses, the oath of fealty was to be compulsory, and appeals from the Irish Free State could be made to the Privy Council.

In the troubled circumstances, it is not surprising that the 1922 election was marked by widespread intimidation and personation. The republicans claimed that the people were being asked only to approve of a coalition government between the two wings of Sinn Féin and that the Treaty was not an issue. However, the results indicated beyond doubt popular approval of the Treaty. Of the 128 seats the pro-Treaty group won 58, the anti-Treaty group 35, Labour 17, Farmers 7, Independent 7 and Dublin University 4. Perhaps the most surprising feature of the election was the extent of the participation of these sectional interests (also to be reckoned as pro-Treaty) and the good showing they made. Of the 620,000 votes cast they had polled between them 247,000, with 239,000 and 134,000 going to the pro- and anti-Treaty groups respectively. In the midst of the political crisis, the electorate was expressing its interest in social and economic issues. Labour, in particular, seemed assured of a role in the new state.

Whatever hope the election results held out of a peaceful political settlement was dashed by the swift course of events. On 22 June Sir Henry Wilson was assassinated in London. Collins's ultimate responsibility for the action has since been asserted but not unnaturally the British government concluded that the assassins, two London-based IRA men, had received their orders from the army executive in the Four Courts though O'Connor denied any involvement. Churchill warned Collins that O'Connor could not 'be permitted to remain with his followers and his arsenal in open rebellion in the heart of Dublin'. It was not, however, British pressure that finally led the provisional government to act, but the daring abduction on 26 June by the Four Courts garrison of General J. J. 'Ginger' O'Connell, Deputy Chief of Staff of the National Army. This was a defiance which could not go unchallenged. Collins and others had been reluctant all along to move against old comrades but Griffith's arguments were now unanswerable. The provisional government, greatly strengthened by the election results, must act quickly or anarchy would prevail. At 3.40 a.m. on 28 June the provisional government in an ultimatum demanded immediate evacuation of the Four Courts by its garrison. Within the hour the National Army attacked the great building with artillery borrowed from British forces still in the Dublin area. Two days later the garrison had surrendered and the fine edifice as well as priceless historical records had been destroyed. The event is usually taken as marking the beginning of the Civil War. Fighting broke out in several city areas, and Cathal Brugha was the first prominent casualty of the conflict. The tortuous manoeuvres for peace were over, the complex alignments simplified, hesitations hardened into firm decisions. Liam Lynch who had done his utmost to prevent the outbreak of fighting now threw in his lot with the Irregulars, as did the anti-Treaty politicians, de Valera hailing the Four Courts garrison as 'the best and bravest of our nation'. The former president's main concern was to keep intact his political leadership over republicans, and his military role in the struggle was a minor one. The oft-repeated accusation by his enemies in subsequent years that he was responsible for the Civil War has little foundation in fact. It was, as we have seen, the military men who set the pace with the politicians following suit. Yet such was de Valera's prestige that had he remained aloof or withdrawn his moral support from the military men, resistance must have crumbled at an early stage. To that extent he cannot avoid a certain measure of responsibility.

The Civil War was primarily a conflict between those tragically divided on constitutional issues, between idealists and pragmatists, between two groups who bitterly accused each other of sabotaging Ireland's independence. Since both the protagonists were products of the Gaelic League and Sinn Féin philosophies, the struggle was hardly one involving different national visions. It was not fought about partition since both sides ardently desired national unity but were equally powerless to achieve it. Still less was it a struggle about social and economic issues: neither Treaty nor anti-Treaty leaders attempted to inject any element of class warfare into the struggle. That is not to say that no social issues were raised by the Civil War. Since the Free State was supported by those who sought a return to order and stability and the protection of property, the alignment sometimes appeared to be along the axis of social class. Conversely the Republicans were supported by an old radical element though it is untrue that all Republicans were men with nothing to lose. As in most civil conflicts, social issues simmered beneath the surface but rarely found unequivocal expression.

At the outset of the ten-months struggle, the Republicans or 'Irregulars' had control of the whole south and west, except for Clare, south Galway and part of Limerick, a city which was of considerable strategic importance. Had it come into republican hands, Irregular forces could be rushed to intervene in the Dublin fighting and the outlook for the provisional government would be serious. However, by the end of July the Irregulars had been forced out of Limerick and the Shannon estuary and fell back on the 'Munster Republic', an area bounded by the sea and a line running from Waterford to Limerick. Waterford fell rather easily to the government forces and so the republican frontier had been breached at its two extremes.

At this stage, before there was a descent into brutality and atrocities, the Labour Party tried to mediate but the provisional government was in no mood for compromise: as they gained control of republican areas they became more determined than ever to crush what they regarded as 'armed revolt'. The Limerick-Tipperary line continued to crumble as Tipperary, Carrick-on-Suir and Clonmel were, in turn, captured, but stiffer resistance was encountered further south. The best fighting material of the Irregulars was still in action then. The numerically larger and better equipped government forces had many untrained and inexperienced men, though stiffened by small groups of the élite Dublin Guards whose participation was an important factor in the government's military success.

In early August the National Army staff accepted General Emmet Dalton's proposal that the republican strongholds of Cork and Kerry should be attacked from the coast and this strategy proved to be very successful. A force which landed at Fenit on the north side of Tralee Bay went on to take Tralee town and over-run north Kerry. Government troops also landed at Passage West in Cork Harbour and fought their way to the city which was quickly evacuated, the Irregulars retreating westwards. By the end of August the republican cause in the field was well and truly lost and the war developed into the familiar guerilla pattern of two years before – flying columns, ambushes, assassinations and booby traps. But now there were two significant differences: the enemies of the Irregulars were thoroughly familiar with local terrain and the Republicans failed to secure the necessary degree of popular support.

Arthur Griffith died on 12 August, the victim of a cerebral haemorrhage. Ten days later, a convoy in which Michael Collins was travelling in the course of an inspection tour in west Cork was ambushed in the lonely valley of Béal na mBláth, near Crookstown, and the Commander-in-Chief was killed at the age of thirty-three. It is probable that the objective, in part at least, of Collins's tour had been to contact republican leaders in an attempt to end the conflict and perhaps to win back their loyalties. His death certainly removed whatever chances of reconciliation still existed.

On 9 September, almost three months after the election, the new Dáil met but was not, of course, attended by the Republican deputies. Cosgrave (as president), the young Kevin O'Higgins (Home Affairs) and Mulcahy (Defence) took over government leadership from their dead colleagues. In October special emergency powers were given to the army to hold military courts and inflict the death penalty for a wide range of offences including the unauthorised possession of arms. These drastic powers would, it was hoped, help to end chaos, limit the widespread destruction and shorten the war: their effect inevitably was to aggravate further an already embittered situation. Meanwhile the Dáil passed the Irish Free State Constitution Bill and on 6 December 1922, exactly one strife-torn year after the signing of the Treaty, the provisional government ceased to exist and the Irish Free State came officially into existence. Republicans refused to recognise the institutions of the new state, claiming that it had usurped the Second Dáil and the Republic. Republican deputies elected de Valera as president of what they alleged was the legitimate government of the Republic. This move was supported by the Army Executive. Of course, the republican government never functioned and the pretence of a rival 'government-in-exile' was gradually and tacitly abandoned. In passing, we may note that the concern of Republicans, then and subsequently, to base their legitimacy on the Second Dáil was in itself an oblique tribute to the strength of the parliamentary tradition in Ireland.

While the Republicans threatened death to those who had voted for the Army Emergency Power resolutions, their enemies carried out a pitiless series of executions. Erskine Childers was executed on 24 November, and on 8 December came the executions of Rory O'Connor, Liam Mellowes, Joseph McKelvey and Dick Barrett in reprisal for the killing of Seán Hales, a pro-Treaty deputy. While the Republicans embarked upon a campaign of sabotage of public services and the destruction of property of ex-Unionists and government supporters in the hope that chaos might further their cause, the government ruthlessly set about breaking the resistance of the Irregulars. By January 1923 over fifty Republicans had been executed and twenty-seven more were to die in the same way before the end of hostilities. The public at large recognised that stern measures were necessary to end the Civil War yet these measures caused some revulsion of feeling which was later to redound to the advantage of Republicans.

By the early spring of 1923, large numbers of Republicans had been captured and the leadership was already aware of the futility of further resistance. The most indomitable of their remaining military men, chief of staff General Liam Lynch, was trapped by Free State forces and fatally wounded on the Knockmealdown mountains on 10 April 1923. His death made a republican ceasefire inevitable, and de Valera tried to secure this on favourable terms. When the government refused to accede to his proposals he issued a proclamation to his followers on 24 May:

> Soldiers of the Republic, Legion of the Rearguard: The Republic can no longer be defended successfully by your arms. Further sacrifice of life would now be vain and continuance of the struggle in arms unwise in the national interest and prejudicial to the future of our cause. Military victory must be allowed to rest for the moment with those who have destroyed the Republic.

Republican arms were dumped and the Irregulars ceased to resist though they were accorded no amnesty and had to go on the run to evade arrest. The Civil War was over.

Compared with the devastating civil conflicts of modern history – American, Spanish, Nigerian – the Irish Civil War seems a small enough affair: the total death-roll for example, did not exceed six or seven hundred. Yet its consequences cannot be measured by the crude criterion of magnitude. The bitterness it engendered and its prolonged consequences on the national life made it as disastrous as greater conflicts elsewhere. The total disorder of the 1922–23 period was a heavy blow to a new political community attempting to lay the foundations of new institutions and a new economy. The promise of great achievement was soured into frustration and cynicism, aggravated by the murderous excesses on both sides. The country was prematurely robbed of talented and dedicated men – Collins, Griffith, Brugha, Childers, Harry Boland, Mellowes and Liam Lynch. A Free State government in 1924, still bearing the scars of the internecine struggle, was in no position to press for a favourable outcome of the Boundary Commission proceedings. The new state with its exaggerated concern for law and order was cast in a dreary conservative mould. For more than a generation the Civil War contributed to the unnatural polarisation of Irish politics around the Treaty issue, while social and economic considerations were relatively neglected. The development of the Labour party and of political parties along normal lines was inhibited. Moreover it is hard not to believe that the language revival movement would have fared very differently had Sinn Féin remained united.

The first general election under the new Irish Free State constitution was held in August 1923: indeed it was the first election since 1910 to be held in anything like normal circumstances. It provided an opportunity of testing popular feeling after the disastrous civil conflict. Despite their abstentionism, their recent total military defeat and their virtually outlawed position, the Republicans secured 44 seats out of 153 and 27.6% of the popular vote: this represented an improvement on their 1922 performance. Clearly, the de Valera appeal was still strong, republicanism was far from being a spent force and recent government ruthlessness was resented. An important ·psychological factor in achieving this result had been the shrewd decision to reorganise anti-Treaty political opinion under the magical name of Sinn Féin, using its constitution and rules and much of its personnel. The pro-Treatyites, organised under Cosgrave in the new Cumann na nGaedheal party launched in April 1923, won 63 seats and wielded political power in the new Dáil which de Valera and his followers refused to recognise. Despite the dominance of the Treaty issue, numerous small groups and individuals had contested the election, attracted by the encouraging prospects proportional representation held out for minorities. Sixteen independent deputies were returned, the Farmers' Union secured 15 seats and the Labour Party 14. The results set the political pattern of the state for many years to come – the divided wings of the 'second' Sinn Féin party sharing the great majority of the seats between them, the sectional interests of Labour and the farmers securing minority representation, and Independents being returned in fairly substantial numbers thanks to proportional representation and to the local, intimate nature of Irish politics. Since farmers and independents, to a greater or lesser extent, supported the government, and since Sinn Féin did not attend the Dáil, it was left to Labour under the leadership of Thomas Johnson and Cathal O'Shannon to perform the valuable democratic service of providing parliamentary opposition.

3 The Irish Free State under Cosgrave, 1923-32

The problems of the Free State government did not end with the cessation of Civil War hostilities. The army's wartime strength of 55,000 was being reduced to 20,000 and discontent was rife among the pro-treaty IRA not only because of demobilisation and its effects but because of other aspects of government policy. Some Army men feared the government was moving away from the Collins view of the Treaty as a stepping-stone to full independence. They wanted more vigorous moves towards a republic and some firm action on partition. They alleged that while they were being pushed into civilian life on small gratuities, 'trucers' and former British Army soldiers were receiving promotion. The upshot was an ultimatum to the government on 24 March 1923: this demanded a move towards a more republican form of government and a suspension of army demobilisation. The 'Army Mutiny', which was an echo of the earlier conflict, was not finally resolved until October and it posed the threat of another round of hostilities. It involved the resignation of two government ministers and of three senior officers from the army council. In the end it was effectively handled by Kevin O'Higgins, the vigorous vice-president of the cabinet or 'Executive Council'. In the event, government control over its military arm was assured and there was upheld the principle of army subordination to the civil power which happily was maintained thereafter.

Another crisis followed quickly on the Army Mutiny. Article XII of the Anglo-Irish Treaty had provided, as we have seen, for the setting up of a Boundary Commission.

Because of the crisis in Ireland over the Treaty and the ensuing civil war, the unstable political situation in England, and, not least, the attempts made to reach a settlement without recourse to the Commission, there was considerable delay in establishing it and this gave the Northern state valuable time to consolidate itself. The Northern Ireland government continued to maintain its very effective 'what-we-have-we-hold' attitude. It claimed it was not bound by the article in question, refused to appoint a commissioner and proposed to ignore all proceedings on the matter. The Irish Free State government, on the other hand, was under pressure from its political opponents to pursue the question and as early as July 1923 selected as its commissioner Eoin MacNeill, an Ulster Catholic from the Glens of Antrim, Minister for Education, distinguished scholar, father figure both of the Gaelic League and the Volunteer movement. Special legislation empowered the English government to appoint in October 1924 J. R. Fisher, a prominent Northern Unionist, as the representative for Northern Ireland. The chairman who was to be neutral between the claims of the two disputants was Justice Richard Feetham of the South African Supreme Court.

The Commission held its first meeting in November 1924. Feetham (who dominated its proceedings) interpreted a vague and ambiguous article to mean that Northern Ireland was to remain substantially 'the same provincial entity' and border adjustments should be 'a mere correction of irregularities'. The wishes of the inhabitants were to be determined, not by a plebiscite, but by consideration of the religious returns of the 1911 census, Catholic being taken to mean 'nationalist' and Protestant 'unionist': 'wishes' were to be interpreted as large majorities in small territorial units. Even so, economic and geographic factors were deemed to outweigh the 'wishes of the inhabitants' so that Feetham found compelling reasons why the nationalist-majority areas of say Derry City and South Down should remain in Northern Ireland. After the Commission had spent some time surveying the border areas, a leak in the *Morning Post* newspaper on 7 November (the evidence points to Fisher as the source of the premature disclosure) forecast that the Commission would make no substantial adjustment of the Border, the only significant transfers being the southern portion of Co. Armagh to the Free State and an important portion of east Donegal to Northern Ireland. MacNeill resigned from the Commission on 20 November since he could not be a party to its forthcoming report. His resignation (followed by his resignation from his government ministry) confirmed what was for nationalists the shock news of the *Morning Post* account and presented the Cosgrave government with a major crisis.

From the standpoint of the Dublin government, the danger now was that the other two Commissioners would go ahead and publish their report which would, by a previous decision of the Privy Council, be legally binding. It was obviously essential to prevent the promulgation of the report and, against a background of urgency and tension, Cosgrave and his ministers together with Craig and British government representatives signed a tripartite agreement in London on 3 December 1925. The powers of the Boundary Commission were revoked, (its report became public only in 1969) the boundary was to remain unchanged, the provisions for a Council of Ireland were in effect abolished but the pious hope was expressed that both Irish governments would discuss matters of mutual interest 'in a spirit of neighbourly comradeship'. The agreement also released the Irish Free State from its liability, under Article V of the Treaty, for part of the British public debt, and it included provisions on responsibility for compensation for malicious damage during the years of conflict.

Predictably, de Valera and his supporters were loud in their recriminations against the Cosgrave government which, they claimed, had given its consent to the dismembering of the country. The Republican leader deplored the cutting off of 'our fairest province': significantly he did not dwell on the tragic separation of Protestant from Catholic, Unionist from Nationalist but rather raised a sentimental lament for the loss of a fourth green field. Regrettably, this was to be the impoverished and sterile tone of anti-partitionism for the next forty years. De Valera and the anti-Treaty deputies could with justice be accused of taking refuge from the painful realities of the problem in a self-righteous dream world of a mystically indivisible 'republic'. They could hardly have been unaware that they also bore a heavy responsibility for the weakness of a government that had no other choice but to accept the continuance of partition.

The debacle of the Boundary Commission brought the reality of partition home to southern Irishmen and, more unpleasantly, to the nationalist minority in the North who had cherished the hope that the arrangements of the Government of Ireland Act would not be lasting. The collapse of the Commission strengthened the IRA in its simplistic conviction that partition could be ended only by force. On the other hand, their own sense of futility in the crisis further increased the growing disenchantment with abstentionism of de Valera and some of his lieutenants, and accelerated their return to constitutional politics.

Meanwhile it was not enough for the Cosgrave administration to survive crises, to avoid the dual dangers of a police state and a military dictatorship, and to proclaim the virtues of parliamentary democracy. The establishment of an efficient police force, an experienced civil service and an impartial judiciary, though admirable in themselves, could hardly be hailed as the building of a new Jerusalem.

A conservative government in every sense and made more so by the support it received from the propertied classes and the large farmers, Cosgrave's administration lacked any real social and economic policy. The notion that it was the government's duty to provide work and redistribute wealth by no means commanded universal acceptance in that period. The halcyon days of agricultural prosperity which benefited merchant as well as farmer were long over and the years of political turmoil from 1921 to 1923 were also ones of economic depression. Agricultural prices continued to drop in the mid-1920s and exports to decline. In an era of free trade, agricultural exports were regarded by government and economic experts alike as the lifeblood of wider economic development: tariff-protection of industries, the central principle of the original Sinn Féin economic philosophy, was frowned upon in the 1920s because it would raise the costs of agricultural exports. State intervention in the economy was limited, tariff protection was infrequent and duties imposed were moderate. Again, in the interests of low agricultural costs, taxes and state expenditure were kept down, budgets were balanced and little was spent on social welfare or on improving the bad housing situation in Dublin and the large towns. In 1924, the old age pension rate was actually cut by a shilling a week! Still, taxation was light and the cost of basic commodities moderate. It suited government policy and the *laissez-faire* economy that emigration which had dropped to a low level during the years of the Great War and the Anglo-Irish struggle was now soaring.

Yet, given the prevailing orthodoxy and conservatism, there were more than modest achievements in some areas. Despite the lack of protection and the global depression in the 1920s the number in industrial employment moved upwards a little – from 103,000 in 1926 to 111,000 in 1931. The Land Act of 1923 was a major stage in the completion of land purchase. The Agricultural Credit Corporation, set up under an Act of 1927 to make credit available for farmers, was of less impact in its immediate operations than in the type of state intervention it prefigured. The sugar beet factory established at Carlow was in time to develop into an important national industry. But the most far-sighted step in the development of native resources by the state was the Shannon Scheme – the beginning of a national supply of electricity – and the establishment of the Electricity Supply Board in 1927, destined to be perhaps the most successful of those semi-state bodies which in future years became characteristic and indispensable features of the Irish economy.

If the domestic policies of the Cumann na nGaedheal administration were, with the exceptions discussed, cautious and unadventurous, the external policy it pursued laid the basis for a constitutional transformation by the

65

time it came to relinquish office in 1932. Its achievements in this sphere though set in a low key were significant. Cumann na nGaedheal was determined to prove Collins right in his 'stepping-stone' view of the Treaty, though in the process it became stamped as a Commonwealth party. The Irish Free State was determined to transcend its limitations as a dominion. This it did by its membership of such international bodies as the League of Nations and the International Labour Organisation as well as by its initiatives in making diplomatic appointments to non-Commonwealth countries. These developments were watched with interest by other Commonwealth countries, especially Canada, which was particularly insistent on the principle of co-equality of the Dominions with Great Britain. Kevin O'Higgins and Desmond Fitzgerald were foremost in formulating this principle at frequent imperial conferences, such as the 1926 conference which laid down that dominions were 'equal in status, in no way subordinate to one another in any aspect of their domestic or external affairs'. A symbol of constitutional evolution was the gradual replacement of the term 'British Empire' by 'British Commonwealth of Nations'. In 1929 it was announced that the Irish Free State would submit international disputes to the Court of International Justice, thus repudiating the notion that disputes between the U.K. and the Dominions were domestic matters. The constitutional refashioning of the Commonwealth reached its culmination in the enactment by the British Parliament in December 1931 of the Statute of Westminster which acknowledged co-equality between Britain and the Dominions and the right of dominion parliaments to repeal or amend Westminster legislation affecting them. Without all this development, the further constitutional changes carried out by de Valera's government from 1932 would not have been possible.

Meanwhile the cause of parliamentary democracy at home had been strengthened by the belated acceptance of the Irish Free State constitutional position by de Valera and his followers. Perhaps the beginnings of that development are to be looked for in the early days after the Civil

War when Gerry Boland and Seán Lemass, two of de Valera's more pragmatic lieutenants, began to be aware of the need to build a political movement combining nationalist and practical appeal. Sinn Féin had done well in the 1923 election but had gone into decline after a period of relative expansion in 1923–24, and its financial resources especially from America began to dry up. Popular support for abstentionism faded and the republican movement could not capitalise on the support it still enjoyed from the small farmers and working class as long as it was committed to the sterile and self-denying policy of remaining in the political wilderness. The Cumann na nGaedheal government was far from being popular but the Irish Free State was a going concern, its laws were being enforced, it was internationally recognised and its citizens were clearly in favour of peace and order. A new policy was imperative to rescue Republicans from their isolation.

At the IRA convention of November 1925, Frank Aiken, chief of staff and a loyal follower of de Valera, admitted that the question of entry into the Free State Dáil was being considered by some members of the republican 'government'. Distrustful of de Valera's intentions and of civil control in general and believing that the Sinn Féin movement had become futile, the IRA withdrew allegiance from the republican 'government' and vested control in its executive body, the Army Council. The IRA secession was not an unmitigated disaster in view of the initiative de Valera was now about to make. The Boundary Commission and the London Agreement of December 1925 brought home to the more perceptive Sinn Féin leaders how helpless they were to influence the course of politics while they remained outside the Free State Dáil.

In March 1926 de Valera put it to the Ard-Fheis of the Sinn Féin organisation of which he was president that 'once the admission oath of the Twenty-six County and Six-County assemblies is removed, it becomes a question not of principle but of policy whether or not Republican representatives should attend these assemblies'. By a narrow majority the Ard-Fheis resolved that it was against Sinn

Féin principles 'to send representatives into any usurping legislature set up by English law in Ireland'. It was the parting of the ways. De Valera immediately resigned from the movement which he had led since its reconstitution in 1917.

Two months later, on 16 May 1926, he launched his new political organisation in Dublin. It was to be called Fianna Fáil ('Warriors of Fál' – a poetic name for Ireland) with the sub-title of 'Republican Party'. The rather strange-sounding name evoked the ancient Irish sagas and, more relevantly, the military side of the recent independence movement, since the initials 'F.F.' had appeared on the Volunteer badge and continued to be used on Free State army uniforms. In broad terms the aims of the party were stated to be 'securing the political independence of a united Ireland as a Republic', the restoration of the Irish language, the development of a native Irish culture, 'the distribution of the land of Ireland so as to get the greatest number possible of Irish families rooted in the soil of Ireland', and, finally, 'the making of Ireland an economic unit as self-contained and self-sufficient as possible with a proper balance between agriculture and other essential industries'. De Valera's view was that while the Dáil was not the legitimate parliament of the Republic it could be used by Republicans to achieve full independence provided they did not have to take the required oath of allegiance, the removal of which therefore became the immediate political objective of the new organisation.

Apart from the great prestige of its leader and the talents of such people as Seán Lemass, Seán T. Ó Ceallaigh, Frank Aiken, Seán MacEntee and James Ryan, Fianna Fáil had the advantage of taking over much of the old Sinn Féin organisation and personnel. Only a small number of the Sinn Féin rank and file did not follow their leader into the new party. In accordance with a profitable Irish custom de Valera went on a successful fund-raising tour of the United States. The great disadvantage from which Fianna Fáil suffered at this stage was that, as an abstentionist party with a civil war past and with continuing ties with the IRA, it was highly suspect to the men of property.

As its first political test approached – a general election was due in 1927 – government actions seemed to play into its hands. In March 1926 Cosgrave had concluded an agreement with the British government which proved highly unpopular at home. This was the 'Ultimate Financial Agreement' which confirmed that the Irish Free State would continue to pay land annuities to Britain and which made Cosgrave's government responsible for the payment of certain RIC pensions: the agreement involved a commitment of about £5m. a year. With its uncompromising policy on law and order, the government brought in a new Public Safety Act, providing for powers of detention and suspension of *habeas corpus,* in response to widespread IRA attacks on police barracks towards the end of 1926. On a slightly more frivolous level, the government incurred further unpopularity by an Intoxicating Liquor Act whose purpose was to reduce the number of licensed premises and limit opening hours.

During the election campaign of June 1927 Fianna Fáil branded its opponents as pro-British, attacked their economic policies and put forward its own attractive combination of constitutional advance and populist economic reform. The new party promised to remove the oath and the shackles of the Treaty, to withhold the land annuities, to transform agricultural society in the interests of tillage and for the benefit of the small farmer, to promote tariff-protected manufacturing industries, and to extend social services while effecting economies in the public service.

The election results could hardly have been more inconclusive. While Cumann na nGaedheal dropped from the 63 seats it had won in 1923 to 46, Fianna Fáil's 44 seats did not constitute any improvement on the Sinn Féin position in 1923. As regards the distribution of the remaining Dáil seats, the results seemed to bear out the views of those who feared that the proportional representation system of election would give rise to a multiplicity of small parties. Labour (22), Farmers (11), National League (8) (a party which catered for residual Redmondite support in the country), Sinn Féin (5) and Independent Republicans (2) all secured representation while 14 independent deputies were elected. On the opening day of the Dáil session de Valera and his followers were refused admission to the assembly because they refused to take the obligatory oath. In the absence of Fianna Fáil, Cosgrave again formed a government with support from farmers and independents but the artificial situation created by the absence of the largest opposition party was soon to be changed with dramatic suddenness.

On 10 July 1927, a fortnight after the opening session of the Dáil, Kevin O'Higgins was assassinated. Vice-President, Minister for Justice and Minister for External Affairs in the new Cosgrave administration, O'Higgins was the strong man of the government and had long been the *bête-noire* of Republicans, though there was never any evidence of republican complicity in his death and de Valera was unequivocal in his condemnation of the murder. The government reacted immediately. A draconian Public Safety Act (to be repealed in December 1928) decreed severe penalties for membership of unlawful associations, provided for drastic search powers and for a special court which could impose death, or life imprisonment, for unlawful possession of firearms. Two other bills were designed to end Fianna Fáil abstentionism and were far-reaching in their consequences. The Electoral Amendment Bill provided that every Dáil candidate should, on nomination, sign an affidavit that, if elected, he would take his seat and take the oath within two months of his election. The penalty for failure to do this was disqualification and vacation of the seat. The second bill deleted the section in the constitution which provided for the initiation of laws or constitutional amendments by the people. Thus all possible methods of circumventing the obstacle of the oath were blocked.

On 11 August 1927 de Valera and his followers signed their names on the book presented to them by the clerk of the Dáil, at the same time affirming they were taking no oath and were simply going through an 'empty formality'. De Valera admitted that 'what we did was contrary to all our former actions . . . our declared policy'. It was a belated, but not an unexpected, denouement on the part of one who, to borrow the phrase of a fellow historian, could well claim to be the constitutional Houdini of his generation. What was of paramount importance, however, was that a turning point had been reached in the history of the new state. Cosgrave must have been aware that his legislation put Cumann na nGaedheal supremacy at risk. The eventual outcome of his statesmanship – and of de Valera's maturity – was the strengthening of parliamentary democracy and the emergence of a stable two-party system.

More immediately the entry of Fianna Fáil into the Dáil created a critical situation for Cosgrave. On 16 August Thomas Johnson, the leader of the Labour Party, moved a vote of no confidence in the government. It seemed likely that a greatly strengthened opposition, comprising Labour and the National League as well as Fianna Fáil, would prevail over Cumann na Gaedheal and its allies among the Farmers and Independents. In this eventuality it was conceivable that Fianna Fáil would support an improbable Labour-National League coalition. But the result of the vote was a tie and the government was spared the ignominy of defeat by the casting vote of the Ceann Comhairle (chairman of the Dáil). However there could be no question of the government attempting to remain in office: parliament was dissolved and another general election called.

The results of the September 1927 election were in marked contrast to that held three months before. The smaller parties, their campaign coffers depleted, suffered severely, Labour and the Farmers losing heavily while Sinn Féin and the National League were virtually wiped out. The Fianna Fáil party which had fought the campaign largely on economic issues (in particular, the matter of the land annuities) increased their parliamentary strength by 13. For the student of Irish electoral history these are significant results. The electorate had checked the centrifugal tendencies of proportional representation: it had reacted unfavourably to the power manoeuvring of the small parties. The government, winning 67 seats, was obviously benefiting from the revulsion over O'Higgins's assassination and the fears of renewed violence which it had aroused. At the same time, the election verdict endorsed Fianna Fáil's decision to enter the field of constitutional politics.

The outcome of the election was that Cosgrave formed another government with the help of the Farmers and some Independents. He stayed in power for an uneasy four and a half years, but his administration became steadily more unpopular with the electorate.

The decline of Cumann na nGaedheal after 1927 is to be explained in terms not only of its unpopular policies but also of its organisational deficiencies. At local level the party depended largely on influential individuals in the larger centres of population and, at election times, on *ad hoc* committees of supporters. Because the organisation was weak and finances low, the party tended to select as candidates well-off farmers, professional and business men – often amateur, part-time politicians. The aura of middle-class respectability which clung to the party especially in the country towns militated against popular support.

In contrast, Fianna Fáil had a remarkably efficient party machine, built up in pursuit of power from the wilderness. The party demonstrated a grasp of political techniques unusual at the period and an appreciation of the concept of mass organisation never approached by its opponents. The Fianna Fáil organisation was built on the basic unit of the *cumann* (association) of which there was one in almost every parish. Harmony was secured at the top by ensuring that the front bench was strongly represented on the national executive. In turn, the national executive always kept in close touch with the cumainn and made sure that local viewpoints were at all times considered. Thus the party strength in the countryside was nourished and rural distrust of Dublin headquarters held in check. The energy and enthusiasm of the voluntary worker, fired by allegiance to de Valera, was a vital ingredient in the party's success. The advanced organisational thinking of Fianna Fáil was indicated by its successful pioneering of an annual church gate collection and by the establishment in 1931 of its own newspaper, *The Irish Press*, to combat a hostile newspaper influence. Fianna Fáil managed to present itself as 'a slightly constitutional party' (Seán Lemass's famous phrase in the Dáil in March 1928) while continuing to identify itself with republican dissent.

From 1927 to 1932 Fianna Fáil in opposition attacked the government along a broad political, economic and social front. A tide of unrest mounted outside parliament as well as inside. Against the background of impoverished living standards, socialist ideas came more into favour in minority republican circles. In 1929 Saor Éire was founded as a radical socialist party under republican patronage. It was condemned by the Catholic hierarchy as 'frankly Communistic'. As republican activities increased so did state repression. There was widespread illegal drilling and a campaign of intimidation of juries in cases where republicans were being tried. Violence and shootings in 1931 were met by the drastic Public Safety Act in October of that year. It set up a military tribunal with power to impose the death penalty, authorised the Executive Council to decide on the illegality of associations and bestowed wide powers of arrest and detention on the police. Saor Éire and the IRA were declared illegal and IRA suspects imprisoned under a cat-and-mouse policy.

There were still many ties in the late 1920s between Fianna Fáil and the IRA, particularly at rank-and-file level and these were further strengthened by the government's repressive policy. The same social classes – small farmers, clerks, labourers – supplied the members of both organisations which had much the same ultimate political objectives. In the Dáil the Fianna Fáil opposition attacked the government policy of political arrests and strongly opposed the public safety measures. De Valera referred sympathetically to the extremist republicans as men 'animated with honest motives' who could 'claim exactly the same continuity that we claimed up to 1925'. Both movements wanted the release of political prisoners and many Fianna Fáil followers joined with Saor Éire members in the campaign against payment of the land annuities. In 1931, Fianna Fáil marched with the IRA in the parade to Tone's grave at Bodenstown, the focus of the annual republican pilgrimage.

During the final years of the Cosgrave administration the economic position deteriorated as the world depression deepened. Exports of meat and dairy produce dropped sharply and there was a big fall in the price of cattle and sheep. Many factories closed and unemployment figures soared. The government attempted to alleviate the crisis by decreasing public expenditure and reducing the salaries of those in public employment, such as gardaí and teachers. These measures further increased the unpopularity of a government whose anti-subversive legislation had already incurred public disapproval. An additional weakening factor was that the government was divided on economic issues, notably on the question of tariffs. In any case it had been in power since the state was founded and there was a widespread desire for political change. Characteristically, not only did Cumann na nGaedheal make no attempt to court popularity with the electorate in an attempt to cling on to power but with almost suicidal stoicism it invited further disaster. It introduced an austerity eve-of-election budget, and prosecuted *The Irish Press* before the military tribunal for seditious libel, a step which simply gave the opposition valuable publicity and won for it considerable public sympathy.

In the election campaign of 1932 the government stressed its achievements in safeguarding the institutions of the state, in maintaining law and order and in effecting economies in the public service. In contrast, Fianna Fáil put forward a policy which, while sounding exciting and dynamic, was calculated to allay the fears of that considerable section of the electorate which still regarded de Valera as a dangerous revolutionary. It was made clear that there would be no violent and radical change in Anglo-Irish relations. It discreetly avoided mentioning the republic while still holding out the ideal of national sovereignty. It emphasised economic self-sufficiency, it promised larger doles and the repudiation of debts to Great Britain. Helped by an intensive organisation, the propaganda of a daily newspaper and the formidable support of many IRA members, the party gained fifteen seats, and with seventy-two deputies was the largest grouping in the new Dáil. Though Cumann na nGaedheal had achieved a pre-election merger with some independents and the remnant of the National League, it still lost ground and was reduced to fifty-seven seats. Labour's support, together with that of three Independents, was sufficient to enable de Valera to form a Fianna Fáil government. Despite rumours of a Free State Army *coup*, the transfer of power was effected smoothly and peacefully, and the new ministers who took office with revolvers in their pockets found that such drastic precautions were after all unnecessary. The coming of their Civil War enemies to power was a bitter pill for men like Cosgrave and Mulcahy but for them there could be no question of interfering with the due process of parliamentary democracy. The 1932 change of government was remarkable not simply because it witnessed the resurgence of a group totally defeated a decade earlier in the Civil War, but because it demonstrated the political maturity and stability of the young state.

4 The Triumph of de Valera, 1932-39

In power, Fianna Fáil set about implementing its programme. One of its first acts was to 'release the prisoners':
the phrase had been an emotive election slogan. The
detested Public Safety Act was revoked and the military
tribunal was abolished. Yet de Valera made it clear that he
had no intention of carrying out that drastic purge of army
and police force which the more extremist of his followers
had been expecting. Within weeks of taking office, the
government brought in a bill to abolish the Oath of
Allegiance, de Valera contending it was a purely domestic
matter. It passed through the Dáil but was held up in the
Senate (a body which de Valera increasingly regarded as
reactionary and obstructive) until May 1933. When the
Oath Bill had gone to the Senate, the government turned
to what was one of the most controversial issues of the
day – the continuing payment of land and other annuities
to the British exchequer. De Valera was determined to
keep these sums in Ireland. The British authorities claimed
that withholding the annuities would violate existing Anglo-
Irish agreements and suggested that recourse might be had
to arbitration. The *principle* of arbitration was acceptable
to the Irish government which insisted however that
adjudication should be on an international rather than on
a Commonwealth basis. No agreement was reached on this
point. The British government and more particularly
J. H. Thomas, the Dominions Secretary (whose irreverent
but memorable description of de Valera was 'the Spanish
onion in the Irish stew') regarded the withholding of the
annuities, together with the removal of the Oath, as an
attack on the whole Treaty settlement. It was because of

this, and not simply to recoup the retained annuities, that the government in London retaliated by imposing a substantial tariff on Irish agricultural produce entering the British market. Counter-measures were taken by Dublin against British imports and the financial-constitutional dispute thus developed into the prolonged 'economic war' between the two countries. During its course, Irish imports were to fall by one-half and Irish exports by three-fifths.

Meanwhile de Valera proceeded to deal with the office of governor-general. The new government set out deliberately to demean the office. In October 1932, James MacNeill was dismissed and replaced by Domhnall Ó Buachalla, 1916 veteran, Irish language enthusiast and follower of de Valera. Ó Buachalla resided not in the viceregal lodge but in a private house, received a greatly reduced salary and never acted in any kind of public or social capacity. His appointment thus paved the way for the total abolition of the office at an opportune moment. In November 1933 constitutional change was taken still further when the governor-general was stripped of his power of withholding assent to bills, and the right of appeal from Irish courts to the privy council in London was terminated.

In the autumn of 1932, the National Centre Party was founded under the leadership of Frank MacDermot and James Dillon. It was essentially a combination of Farmers and Independents and it was an attempt to give strength and cohesion to those who were vitally concerned with the damaging effects of the Economic War on the economy. It was pledged to end this conflict, to remove Civil War bitterness and to try to secure all-Ireland unity by a conciliatory Northern policy – a singularly enlightened view in the Ireland of the 1930s.

As moves were being contemplated to bring about a united opposition front to Fianna Fáil, de Valera suddenly dissolved the Dáil early in January 1933. The decision to precipitate a seemingly unnecessary and politically hazardous mid-winter election disconcerted most of his ministers but his political prescience and flair for timing were to be vindicated – not for the only time – by the outcome. He wanted a strong mandate for his policies in the tough struggle that lay ahead with the British and with his political opponents at home. The 'snap' election was also designed to head off the incipient moves for a united front among the opposition, and an overall majority could enable him to dispense with his reliance on the Labour Party. The election campaign was bitter and violent and the issues of the Civil War were given a new lease of life. Cosgrave and his party denounced the retention of the annuities and the constitutional changes as a violation of the national honour while Fianna Fáil took its stand on a much stronger and more popular principle – the right of a small nation to free itself from imperial ties. Its accusations that its opponents were damaging the national interest were effective. The intense public interest was reflected in the record 81 per cent turnout of the electorate. While the new Centre Party won 11 seats, Labour 8 and the Independents 9, the real contest was between de Valera and Cosgrave. Cumann na nGaedheal dropped to 48 seats while Fianna Fáil reached 77. It could now count on an overall majority – albeit by the slenderest of margins – the first party to do so in the history of the state. The result not only confirmed the personal ascendancy of de Valera in Irish politics: despite the continuing background turbulence, it also made for a central stability in Irish political life.

In February 1932 the Army Comrades Association was founded. In origin, it was an organisation of ex-Free State Army members. Its beginnings were uncontroversial and its principal objective seemed to be the promotion of its members' welfare, especially those in need. In August 1932 the leadership of the movement was taken over by Dr T. F. O'Higgins (brother of the assassinated Kevin O'Higgins) who announced that a volunteer body would be set up. By the end of the year, the Association had established itself very quickly as an important political force. The reason for its rapid expansion and for its new character was the

growing fear among members of the Cumann na nGaedheal and the National Centre parties that Fianna Fáil and
the IRA were determined to deprive opposition speakers of
the rights of free speech and assembly. Concern was also
expressed over Fianna Fáil exercise of patronage, and what
was termed the growing menace of Communism, though
the element of Communism within or without the IRA was
negligible. It was true that political meetings were broken
up by Republicans who loudly condemned 'Cosgraveite
traitors'. Regarding the gardaí and military as unable to
afford them adequate protection, Cumann na nGaedheal
came to rely on the Army Comrades Association to supply
ex-ministers with bodyguards at public meetings and
guarantee them a hearing. By the end of 1932 O'Higgins
was claiming that the Association numbered 30,000 men.
During the 1933 election there were several sharp clashes
between the ACA and their opponents. In April 1933 the
blue shirt began to appear as the distinctive uniform of
the movement (hence the popular description 'Blueshirts').
This, it was hoped, would heighten the sense of comradeship as well as serve the very practical purpose of avoiding
clashes between members unknown to one another. The
opponents of the ACA regarded the new development as
further evidence of the sinister right-wing nature of the
movement.

In February 1933, just after his re-election de Valera dismissed Eoin O'Duffy from his position as commissioner
of the Gardaí, ostensibly because the government lacked
'full confidence' in him. General O'Duffy was a colourful
and ebullient figure with a spectacular army career behind
him. His abrupt dismissal was taken by Cosgraveites as
further evidence that the police force could no longer be
relied upon for protection. In July, O'Duffy took over the
leadership of the ACA which now aimed at social and
economic reform along corporate lines and was renamed
the National Guard.

Late in July, O'Duffy announced that he would lead the
National Guard on 13 August in the annual commemora-
tive parade to Leinster Lawn, (fronting parliament build-

ings) in honour of Collins, Griffith and Kevin O'Higgins. At a day's notice, the government banned the parade. The fact was that the IRA had already threatened to attack the Blueshirt marchers and that the parade would almost certainly cause a serious breach of the peace resulting in bloodshed. The government also wanted to assert its authority against a strong quasi-military force before it should become too menacing. O'Duffy accepted the ban and, as a consequence, suffered some loss of face. But, as with the Repeal movement in 1843, the Blueshirts survived this crisis and were far from being a spent force. Provincial parades were held a week later in defiance of a government ban and this resulted in the proclamation of the National Guard and the reconstitution of the military tribunal. These strong government measures precipitated the merger, in September 1933, of the banned National Guard, the National Centre party and Cumann na nGaedheal in a new party under O'Duffy's presidency. This was to be called the United Ireland Party or *Fine Gael*, the name by which it became generally known. Its policy was declared to be 'the voluntary reunion of all Ireland in a single state as a member, without abatement of sovereignty, of the British Commonwealth of Nations in free and equal partnership'. The National Guard was reconstituted within the Fine Gael organisation as the Young Ireland Association whose members would still wear blue shirts and who would continue to be led by O'Duffy as director-general. When in the following December the Young Ireland Association was also banned, it was replaced by the League of Youth. In the spring of 1934 the government introduced a bill to prohibit the wearing of uniforms : it was passed in the Dáil after a bitter debate but it was refused a second reading by the Senate as violating the principle of free expression of opinion. By the time the statutory period elapsed for the Dáil to reconsider the bill, the Blueshirt movement was already in the process of disintegration and the measure was no longer necessary. But the Senate's action helped to seal that body's doom : it had long been regarded by de

Valera as obstructionist and he now took immediate steps to have it abolished.

It is true to say that the parliamentary chiefs of Cumann na nGaedheal had chosen O'Duffy as their leader because they hoped to return to political power on the wave crest of his popularity. They were soon to repent of their choice. Volatile and temperamental, he frequently made public utterances which his colleagues found embarrassing. Despite his predictions of sweeping success, the local elections of June 1934 showed that Fine Gael was far from being on the road back to power. In reality the Blueshirts could make capital only of one issue – the adverse impact of the Economic War on the large farmers or cattle ranchers of the midlands and south whose cattle were impounded for non-payment of annuities and rates, and auctioned at little more than nominal prices. Blueshirts helped farmers to resist the authorities in seizing and auctioning their cattle. Fine Gael parliamentary leaders felt increasingly uneasy at the growth of this illegality and violence. In August 1934 the first annual congress of the League of Youth called on farmers to refuse the payment of land annuities to the government. Dissatisfaction with O'Duffy's leadership came to a head and his statements were disowned by responsible elements within Fine Gael. Late in August, Professor James Hogan (the Blueshirt movement's leading intellectual) resigned from the Fine Gael executive in protest against O'Duffy's 'generally destructive and hysterical leadership'. Within weeks O'Duffy himself unexpectedly resigned – more correctly, perhaps, was ousted – from the leadership, citing irreconcilable differences of policy between himself and his colleagues. There followed a period of confusion and division and by the end of the year the Blueshirts were in considerable disarray. They were in part the victim of their own dissensions but their decline was also hastened by tougher government measures on agrarian disturbances as well as by the 'coal-cattle' pact, concluded in January 1935 between the British and Irish governments. This somewhat mollified farming discontent by increasing the quota of cattle for export.

O'Duffy's final dramatic phase of activity was the organisation of an Irish brigade in the autumn of 1936 to fight on Franco's side in the Spanish Civil War. Meanwhile, Fine Gael, purged of its extra-parliamentary activities, returned to orthodox constitutional opposition. Cosgrave had been elected president at the party ard-fheis in March 1935, and relations noticeably improved between the opposition and the government in that year. Its brief alliance with a militarist wing had damaged the prestige of the Fine Gael party and was a factor in its further decline.

Blueshirtism to its opponents, was the Irish counterpart of fascism, and a grave threat to democracy. Yet such ideology as it had was inspired less by Mussolini's fascism than by the social teaching of Pope Pius XI on vocational organisation which enjoyed considerable vogue with Irish Catholic thinkers then and thereafter, finding expression indeed in parts of de Valera's new constitution and in the structure of the new Senate. It is true that O'Duffy in his later period made no secret of his admiration for fascism but all the evidence is that the Blueshirts were influenced more by the outward forms of fascism than by its inner spirit. Certainly all the liturgical trappings were there – parades, salutes, uniforms – and perhaps *some* of the characteristics. The Blueshirts were vigorous supporters of that hysterical anti-Communism to be found in bishops' pastorals, in sermons and in the conservative press of the 1930s. However, the Blueshirts differed notably in at least two vital respects from their continental counterparts: firstly, their readiness to give 'ten blows for every one received' was a far cry from that essential belief in *systematic* violence which was the hall-mark of continental forms of fascism; secondly, the Blueshirts repeatedly proclaimed their belief in democracy and asserted that their corporatist ideas, far from conflicting with democratic institutions, would develop and strengthen them. In the last analysis, Blueshirtism was essentially an Irish phenomenon, adding colour to the drabness of life in the 1930s. Its conflict with the Fianna Fáil government was less a clash between fascism and democracy than a relatively bloodless restaging of the civil conflict of the previous decade, brought about by the dramatic circumstances in which Fianna Fáil had come to power.

As the Blueshirt movement disintegrated, de Valera's government found itself having to come to grips with a far more formidable extra-parliamentary threat. The honeymoon between Fianna Fáil and the IRA lasted for some time after 1932 particularly while the Blueshirts had to be faced as the common enemy. But the relationship had deteriorated sharply by the end of 1934, and by 1935 the republican organ *An Phoblacht* was directing the bitter invective once reserved for Cumann na nGaedheal against the erstwhile allies of the IRA.

An Phoblacht made it clear that the severance of 'some of the imperial tentacles like the Oath and the governor-generalship' did not mean that true republicans could 'give allegiance to a cabinet which accepts or functions within the British Empire'. Agrarian radicals wanted a different solution to the land annuities question from that proposed by Fianna Fáil. And the policy of industrial tariffs seemed to some sections of radical republicanism to be simply a shoring-up of Irish capitalism. De Valera's refusal to carry out a purge of 'traitors' was a further source of disillusion.

Within the IRA itself there was a basic divergence of view between the 'traditionalists' and the 'socialists'. The former held that any revolutionary social changes must await the establishment of the Republic while the others such as Peadar O'Donnell and George Gilmore argued that republicans must involve themselves in the social and economic struggles of the people and thus win back the support of workers and small farmers who had been lured away by Fianna Fáil. These conflicting views led to a split among republicans in 1934 when the dissident socialists broke away to attempt the formation of a republican congress, intended to be a rallying force of workers and small farmers. Despite promising beginnings it never became a reality and was itself rent by dissension. Its last act was to organise support for the anti-Franco forces in Spain and a unit of 120 volunteers suffered severe casualties.

The removal of the Oath and of other constitutional restrictions went a long way towards conciliating republican sentiment in the country at large, leaving only the extremists dissatisfied. The awarding of pensions to anti-Treatyites also made inroads on republican support while the setting up by the government in 1934 of a volunteer reserve force provided a harmless safety valve for military ardour.

The IRA's clashes with the Blueshirts seemed to tarnish their high purpose and suggested a gangster image. As an armed, secret and violent movement, the organisation found that public sympathy was more and more withdrawn from it especially when it was associated with killings such as those of Richard More O'Ferrall in February 1935 and Admiral Somerville in March 1936. The doctrines of militarism palled in a decade surfeited with violence. Public opinion, too, had grown accustomed, from government action against the Blueshirts, to the notion that it was the state's right and duty to deploy force firmly against extremists. In this climate of opinion it was not difficult for the government to use against the IRA the same machinery of state repression it had set up against the Blueshirts, especially the use of the special police and the revived military tribunal. In June 1936 the IRA was proclaimed an illegal body and its chief of staff imprisoned. It now seemed that de Valera had put paid to the threat from the left just as he had dealt with the forces of the right: in fact, the IRA proved to be a particularly troublesome ghost to lay.

'The Ireland we dreamed of would be the home of a people who valued material wealth only as the basis of a right living, of a people who were satisfied with a frugal comfort and devoted their leisure to the things of the spirit'. De Valera's unworldly vision, here expressed in his 1943 St. Patrick's Day speech, did him no political harm: meanwhile, his more pragmatic lieutenants went ahead with the attempt to implement Fianna Fáil social and economic policy. Here too perhaps there was naiveté, though of a different kind, as when Seán Lemass, party spokesman on economic matters and later the architect of the country's economy for thirty years, confidently proclaimed in 1928 his belief in self-sufficiency. This was the economic nationalism of Griffith and Sinn Féin and indeed of an older lineage. In agriculture, it meant an encouragement of tillage and in industry the development of native manufactures: overall, it was intended to create employment and thus decrease emigration.

When Fianna Fáil came to power in 1932 there was developed a system of control of imports and a wide range of tariffs so that home industries could grow behind protective walls. Such industries were to be further encouraged by incentives like the Control of Manufactures Act 1932–34, the setting up of the Industrial Credit Company in 1933 and the extension of trade loans which had been begun as far back as 1924. But because of the lack of private capital and the legendary caution of Irish investors the state felt itself increasingly called upon to help economic and other activity by the creation of a wide variety of state-sponsored bodies. The trend had begun in the 1920s, notably with electricity generation, and was intensified under Fianna Fáil. The better-known of the nineteen state-sponsored bodies set up between 1927 and the outbreak of World War II included the Electricity Supply Board, the Industrial Credit Company, the Agricultural Credit Corporation, the Irish Sugar Company, Aer Lingus, the Irish Life Assurance Company, Bord Fáilte Éireann and the Hospitals' Trust Board.

In agriculture the task was formidable. Against a background of world depression and Anglo-Irish economic war, agricultural exports had plummetted. In this sphere, self-sufficiency was pursued by decreasing dependence on the cattle industry while giving maximum encouragement to home-grown produce and feeding stuffs. A guaranteed price was laid down for wheat; export subsidies were given for butter, bacon and other commodities; controls were exercised on imported foodstuffs; a beet-sugar industry was promoted; and land annuity charges, payable to the Dublin exchequer, were halved.

Was self-sufficiency a delusion in the 1930s? Net industrial output increased by 44 per cent from 1931 to 1938 while the numbers in industrial employment in the same period increased from 111,000 to 166,000. But industrial exports fell by one-third over the same period since home industries were too small in scale to develop proper export outlets, and relatively high wages and interest rates meant that Irish goods could not economically compete. But what made industrial self-sufficiency particularly elusive was that an Irish industrial economy was dependent on imported fuel, machinery and raw materials. Industrial protection also ran the risk of carrying the burden of inefficient and slothful, if not corrupt, manufacturers. Yet the establishment of tariff-created industries gave new employment opportunities in rural areas and achieved the beginnings of managerial training.

In agriculture, the most impressive aspect seemed to be the spectacular growth in the area under wheat, from 21,000 acres in 1931 to 255,000 acres in 1936. The campaign for home-grown wheat was a controversially political one and the value of the policy was soon to be appreciated. Yet the twelve-fold increase in wheat production was at the expense of other tillage crops. The swing to tillage decreased as the cattle trade began to reassert itself when the coal-cattle pact of 1935 held out hopeful indications. The traditional patterns of Irish agriculture had not, after all, been drastically changed, and rural depopulation proceeded.

It is impossible to consider the economic history of the 1930s in isolation from the Economic War. Protection would have been the Fianna Fáil policy in any case but the Economic War reinforced protectionist trends and at the same time militated against the success of the government's economic policy in every sphere. The most obvious impact of the dispute was on the livestock industry: cattle exports fell from 775,000 in 1929 to 500,000 in 1934. A general fall in incomes contributed to a rise in emigration in the late 1930s and this added to the general decrease in the demand for Irish goods.

Fianna Fáil never set out to transform Irish society totally. Its policy was mildly progressive but by later standards its approach to social reform was very moderate. The Housing Act of 1932 provided for generous state subventions for house building schemes operated by local authorities. The building of 132,000 houses in the decade after 1932 was not only an advance in essential living standards but also an important source of employment. In social welfare, more liberal criteria were adopted for the awarding of blind and old-age pensions. Unemployment assistance was introduced in 1933 and widows' and orphans' pensions in 1935. However modest these advances may be considered, they were certainly more enlightened than the conservative approaches which continued to prevail in the fields of education and health.

Political and constitutional changes were much more spectacular. De Valera's objective was not, as he made clear to extremist republicans, a dramatic declaration of the Republic which might create considerable complications – North-South, Anglo-Irish and international. Rather did he wish to remove 'any form or symbol that is out of keeping with Ireland's right as a sovereign nation . . . so that this state that we control may be a Republic in fact: and that, when the time comes the proclaiming of the Republic may involve no more than a ceremony, the formal confirmation of a status already attained.' After the removal of the Oath of Allegiance, the stultification of the role of the governor-general and the abolition of the right of appeal from the Irish courts to the privy council in London, the extensive changes wrought to the existing constitution by both Cumann na nGaedheal and Fianna Fáil administrations obviously necessitated the drafting of a new basic document for the state. King Edward VIII was informed in June 1936 that a new constitution would 'deal with the internal affairs of Saorstát Éireann, leaving unaffected the constitutional usages relating to external affairs.'

The abolition of the Senate in May 1936 made it easier to enact important legislation later that year when the government took advantage of the abdication crisis in England to define anew the Anglo-Irish constitutional relationship. The Dáil was specially summoned to meet on 11 December 1936, the day of Edward VIII's abdication. Assured of a Dáil majority and no longer troubled by what a second chamber might do, the government introduced two bills together with a guillotine motion whereby all stages would be completed by the following night. The Constitution (Amendment No. 27) Bill removed all references to the king and the governor-general in the existing Free State constitution. The second bill – the Executive Authority (External Relations) Bill – provided that as long as Ireland was associated with the Commonwealth 'and so long as the King recognised by these nations as the symbol of their co-operation continues to act on behalf of each of those nations . . . for the purpose of the appointment of diplomatic and consular representatives, and the conclusion of international agreements, the King so recognised may, and is hereby authorised to, act on behalf of Saorstát Éireann for the like purposes, as and when advised by the Executive Council to do so.' By the passage of these acts de Valera had taken an important step towards achieving the principle of external association which had been his alternative to the dominion status of the Anglo-Irish Treaty of 1921. By the External Relations Act which was to govern Anglo-Irish constitutional relations for the next twelve years, de Valera hoped to satisfy separatist sentiments while avoiding a direct challenge to Britain, and by retaining the king in foreign affairs he preserved a tenuous link with the Commonwealth which he hoped would be of help at some future stage in the reunification of Ireland.

The new constitution took shape during 1936 and early 1937. De Valera consulted a number of interests, notably Catholic and other churchmen, but the document must be regarded as very much his own creation. After a theatrical preamble which invoked 'the name of the Most Holy Trinity from whom is all authority', the first article proceeded to make a ringing declaration of popular sovereignty – 'the Irish nation hereby affirms its inalienable, indefeasible, and sovereign right to choose its own form of Government, to determine its relations with other nations, and to develop its life, political, economic and cultural, in accordance with its own genius and traditions.' There was no reference throughout to king or commonwealth; equally, the term 'republic' nowhere appeared. (In de Valera's view, the use of 'republic' could be justified only if the state had jurisdiction over the whole of Ireland.) The name of the state was to be 'Éire, or in the English language, Ireland'. The national territory was defined as 'the whole island of Ireland, its islands and the territorial seas' (Art. 2) but 'pending the re-integration of the national territory . . .' the laws of the state would apply only to the Irish Free State area (Art. 3). The head of state was to be a popularly-elected President whose duties would be mainly formal. The government was to be headed by a *taoiseach* or prime minister whose prerogatives and initiatives were obviously intended to be stronger than those of the president of the executive council under the old constitution. A bicameral *oireachtas* of *dáil* and *seanad* was restored and representation in the Senate was envisaged along professional or vocational lines. Effectively the powers of the Senate were restricted to delaying Dáil legislation for a stated period. Regular elections to the Dáil would be held – citizens over twenty-one voting on a proportional representation system. The constitution also provided for the holding of referenda. The machinery of law and justice would continue largely as before. In the sections dealing with fundamental rights, citizens were guaranteed freedom of expression, assembly and association 'subject to public order and morality'. The state would endeavour to ensure 'that mothers shall not be obliged by economic necessity to engage in labour to the neglect of their duties in the home' (Art. 41.). The institution of marriage would be guarded 'with special care', and 'no law shall be enacted providing for the grant of a dissolution of marriage' (Art. 41.). The right 'to the private ownership of external

89

goods' was acknowledged. Under Article 44, the state acknowledged 'that the homage of public worship is due to Almighty God. It shall hold His Name in reverence, and shall respect and honour religion'. One sub-section of this article was to become the subject of some controversy since it afforded recognition by the state of 'the special position' of Roman Catholicism as the religion of 'the great majority of the citizens'. But Article 44 also guaranteed 'freedom of conscience and the free profession and practice of religion . . . subject to public order and morality'. Similarly there would be no state endowment of religion and no imposition of disabilities or discrimination 'on the ground of religious profession, belief or status'.

The 1937 Constitution attempted to give expression to two very different notions – the liberal and secular tradition of parliamentary democracy *and* the concept of a state grounded upon Catholic social teaching. On the one hand, there was the assertion of the political culture which Sinn Féin had, in a sense, inherited from the old Irish party: on the other, there was the Irish reflection of the contemporary ideas of Catholic sociologists with particular reference to the then fashionable principles of vocationalism. It must be remembered that from the 1930s to the 1950s the idea persisted that Catholic social principles could be applied successfully to Irish secular life and so help create a Christian society. In fact, Irish Catholicism continued to remain a private and devotional religion which had little relevance to the cold, amoral world of commerce and industry and politics.

The criticisms of the Constitution which were voiced a generation later did not exist significantly in 1937 or rather the document was criticised on quite different grounds. Indeed, it was hailed in some quarters as a tolerant and liberal document and proved to be a model for the constitution makers of Burma a decade later! At home, the main concern of de Valera's political opponents was that the 'strange' new office of the presidency was designed to give more scope to his ambition and increase his power. In fact, de Valera envisaged the president as the guardian of the people's rights. Feminists complained that Art. 41 reflected the prejudices of a patriarchal society and was intended to convey that 'woman's place was in the home'. The anti-divorce clause, though criticised by the tiny band of indomitable liberals who never accepted the insularity and oppressiveness of post-independence Ireland, evoked no real protest in a homogeneously Catholic society. The Protestant minority, for their own reasons, had accepted the values of the Catholic state, and Article 44 was apparently acceptable to the leaders of all denominations. Its most vociferous critics at the time were those Catholic zealots represented by the lunatic fringe styling itself Maria Duce, which complained that the article was *too* liberal!

A puzzling feature of the Constitution was the decision to restore the bicameral system, in spite of the trouble which the old Senate had created for de Valera from the time of his accession to power. The hope that the new apolitical Senate would represent a valuable cross-section of Irish vocational talents soon proved illusory, and that undistinguished assembly became a nursing home for defeated political veterans as well as a grooming stable for hopeful young aspirants. The clause which made Irish the first official language of the state, taken in conjunction with government inaction on the problems of the Gaeltachts, and its inertia in language policy generally, made a large contribution to the double-think and hypocrisy which always characterised the state's policy on language restoration.

But the really basic contradiction in the Constitution reflected a deep-rooted ambivalence in Irish nationalist thinking. Articles 2 and 3 expressed the historic aspirations of Irish nationalists to unity, yet in many respects the Constitution bore a specifically Catholic complexion, expressing the values of a homogeneously Catholic Twenty-Six County society. This being so, it was understandable that the affirmation of Irish unity could be interpreted by Ulster Unionists as a claim of territorial aggrandisement by the Catholic state over the Protestant north-east.

Despite opposition from Fine Gael in its role of a Commonwealth party and from Labour (which would have preferred a clear-cut republican position), the Constitution was approved by the Dáil on 14 June 1937 and was then submitted to the electorate. De Valera, whose paternalism was quite consistent with a genuine concern for the democratic process, was emphatic that the basic instrument of the state would be enacted by the people and derive its authority from the popular will. It was to be put to the people on the same day as a general election, on 1 July 1937. Though de Valera appealed for a consideration of the Constitution on its merits, he was very well aware that it would for the most part be a party issue; it was essential, then, that it should be approved by a large number of voters.

The result indicated that, after all, a substantial section of the people *did* consider the instrument on its merits. Sixty-five per cent of the electorate expressed their opinion on the Constitution: it was approved by 685,105 votes to 526,945, that is, 57 per cent of those who voted favoured its enactment, while only 45.3 per cent of the poll at the general election went to Fianna Fáil. The party's strength was reduced to 69 seats out of a 138-strong Dáil. Since it was still by far the largest party, it again formed a government with Labour support. The loss of its overall majority could be attributed to the controversial and turbulent events of the previous four years and particularly perhaps to the disastrous impact of the Economic War on an economy that was depressed to begin with.

The Constitution automatically came into force on 29 September 1937. The British government subsequently declared that the constitutional change did not affect Irish membership of the Commonwealth. On 4 May 1938 the first President of the state was elected unopposed. He was Douglas Hyde, a Protestant, whose avowedly non-political work for the Gaelic League had ironically made an incalculable contribution to the founding of an independent Irish state.

Moves for a general settlement of Anglo-Irish differences

had been afoot for some considerable time, and matters were greatly helped by the good relationship established between de Valera and Malcolm MacDonald, Thomas's successor as Dominions Secretary in the English cabinet. Now that the new Constitution was safely in operation, an Anglo-Irish *rapprochement* would further stabilise Irish politics and would in a general way be desirable in the face of the growing threat of a European war. From an Irish standpoint what was at issue was not merely the ending of an injurious economic struggle but also the partition question as well as the continuing occupation of Irish ports by British forces. During the Treaty debates only Erskine Childers had fully grasped that such occupation would make independence illusory. A state which relinquished control of any of its harbours to another power could not possibly hope to adopt an independent role in an international conflict. Moreover, under the Anglo-Irish Treaty of 1921, Britain could claim *additional* facilities in this regard.

In January 1938, vital talks commenced in London, with an Irish delegation under de Valera facing an English team led by Neville Chamberlain, the prime minister. De Valera made the Irish priorities clear – the abolition of partition, the handing over of the Treaty ports and the ending of the crippling duties on Irish goods. The satisfaction of these demands would, he claimed, considerably benefit Britain as well, since Ireland could then make proper provision for its own defence and ensure that the country would not be used as a base of attack against Britain. For their part, the British negotiators planned to link any concessions with a defence agreement between the two countries. De Valera pushed hard on the partition issue, arguing its inherent injustice, emphasising Unionist discrimination against the nationalist minority in Northern Ireland and asserting that while partition lasted no Dublin government could sign a defence agreement with Britain. When Chamberlain was adamant that there could be no question of London putting pressure on Belfast, it became painfully clear to de Valera that there would be no concessions on partition. He rejected a British suggestion that the Dublin government should open the Twenty-Six county market to Six-County products: as long as the Stormont government treated its minority unjustly he saw no reason why it should be given free entry to the Irish market. De Valera's approach to the 'partition' question, in particular his assumption that it was primarily a matter for Britain to resolve, remained consistently inadequate throughout his political career and demonstrated his repeated failure to comprehend the complexity of the Irish unity issue.✕

When it was accepted by both sides that no progress was possible in certain fields – partition, a defence agreement, special trade concessions to Northern Ireland – more fruitful discussion was continued in other areas. Three agreements were signed on 25 April 1938 and published on the following day. By the first agreement, Articles 6 and 7 of the Anglo-Irish Treaty of 1921 were abrogated. Not only was British control over naval bases at Cobh, Lough Swilly and Berehaven relinquished but the claim to naval and military facilities exercisable under those articles was unreservedly revoked. Chamberlain, acting on the advice of the Chiefs of Staff, presumably considered the cession of the ports a worthwhile price to pay for Irish friendliness.

The second agreement effectively ended the Economic War. Against the initial British claim of £104 million, it was agreed that Ireland should pay £10 million as a final financial settlement of all points at issue between the two countries, including the British claim to payment of land annuities. The special duties imposed by both governments at the outset of the quarrel were abolished.

The third agreement was a trade arrangement whereby the British market was to be opened again to the Irish cattle trade and to Irish food products. Irish manufacturers could sell their products in the United Kingdom with few restrictions. In return, Ireland undertook to review existing tariffs and certain British goods were given duty-free access to the Irish market, but Irish industries 'not fully established' would continue to be given protection.

The Anglo-Irish agreements of 1938 can fairly be

described as a triumph for the Irish side and it is important to stress their significance in the history of the Irish state, in Anglo-Irish relations and indeed in de Valera's political career. The trade agreement recognised the close bonds of the British and Irish economies while leaving Ireland free to develop its own industrial resources. World War II intervened before the implications of the agreement could be worked out but there was certainly some substance in the Fine Gael taunt that Fianna Fáil was moving towards free trade and modifying its original policy of industrial protection. The settlement of the vexed annuities questions was an Irish victory, though it did not seem so to those champions of agrarian justice who believed annuities should not be paid to *any* government. Equally disenchanted were those who believed, and were to continue believing in the years ahead, that 'de Valera's economic war' had greatly aggravated the endemic poverty and depression of rural Ireland.

But it was the handing back of the ports that constituted the greatest gain of the 1938 agreements. It was the culmination, and a tangible one, of the remarkable evolution of the Irish Free State from shackled dominion status to sovereignty, a process well begun with Cosgrave's administration and spectacularly developed under de Valera. The return of the ports made independence of action a reality: nothing else would have made neutrality feasible.

The Anglo-Irish agreements of 1938 mark a new phase in Anglo-Irish *détente*: the political leader of the anti-Treaty forces had achieved a new respectability at home and in Britain: his piecemeal undoing of the Treaty was acclaimed in nationalist Ireland and accepted, if not welcomed, in imperial Britain.

More immediately, the agreements redounded to the domestic credit of Fianna Fáil. Not for the first or last time de Valera was determined to exploit a favourable opportunity to retrieve his overall majority in the Dáil. In May 1938, his government was defeated by a single vote on a minor matter by a combination of Fine Gael, Labour and Independent deputies. Here was the welcome pretext for securing an immediate dissolution of the Dáil. With an organisation far outstripping its rivals and with the achievements of the Anglo-Irish agreements still glossy, Fianna Fáil was very favourably placed. True, unemployment and poverty were still rife but much could be made of the expected benefits that would flow from the reopening of the British markets. Fine Gael, already dogged by the backward look and discomfited by the London agreements, gave the unfortunate impression that its main policy was the complaint that its clothes had been stolen. The outcome was Fianna Fáil's greatest election triumph, 52 per cent of the popular vote and an overall majority of 15 seats. Given the built-in checks of a proportional representation system, this was a sweeping victory and it represented a percentage of the total poll never again to be approached. Fianna Fáil's independence of Labour was now assured, and de Valera's hand was enormously strengthened in dealing with the IRA and in the formulation and execution of an effective neutrality policy. The Dáil elected in 1938 was to survive for its full constitutional term and was to be the longest Dáil in the history of the state.

It was hoped that the dismantling of the Treaty at so many points, the enactment of the new Constitution and the return of the British-held ports would undermine the *rationale* of illegal republican activity. The hope proved illusory. For Seán MacBride, a former IRA chief of staff, the 1937 Constitution rationalised or legitimised the state: for most of his comrades the Dublin administration still remained a usurpation of the betrayed Republic, and the failure of the 1938 agreements to deal with partition simply confirmed their conviction that only direct action could reunite the country. The IRA rallied in 1938 and showed signs of fresh life as men went into training and British customs huts along the border were destroyed. In December 1938 the 'Executive Council of Dáil Éireann' that is, the Second Dáil, vested its authority in the IRA Army Council, and differences between the civilian and military branches of the republican movement were mini-mised. Henceforth the IRA Army Council was the supreme executive authority.

On 12 January 1939, an IRA ultimatum was delivered to Lord Halifax, the British Foreign Secretary, demanding the withdrawal within four days of all British forces, civil and military, from Irish soil: otherwise the IRA would take 'appropriate action'. There thus began the bombing incendiary raids in England. This IRA strategy (to be financed, classically, through Clan na Gael) of carrying out warlike action on English soil recalled the Fenian dynamite campaign of the late nineteenth century. Apparently the IRA hoped that the campaign would exacerbate Anglo-Irish relations to the point where a resumption of the ancient conflict would be inevitable. In fact, de Valera believed the bombing campaign ended any hopes of an effective anti-partition agitation in England, though he was to inform Chamberlain that violent protests could only be expected as long as partition continued. In the IRA itself there was a division in the leadership over the decision to proceed with the bombing campaign, the opponents of the plan feeling that action might more appropriately be taken in Northern Ireland. In any case, the IRA shared the fatal shortcomings of de Valera in regard to the unity question, as indeed did the whole post-Treaty nationalist generation. It was a common and persis-tent fallacy to suppose that partition could be undone by pressuring Britain.

IRA members were given elementary instruction on bomb-making but their effectiveness as incendiaries re-mained limited. The campaign was intended to be one of terror and intimidation as well as an instrument of sabo-tage against power-grids, stations and factories. Though the aim was to destroy property without taking life, the plant-ing of bombs in telephone boxes, lavatories and railway stations was bound to result in fatal casualties. The tragic climax came on 25 August 1939 in Coventry. A bomb on a bicycle-carrier exploded in the crowded Broadgate, killing five people and wounding seventy. The outrage shocked peacetime England.

That the campaign lost momentum after Coventry was due not only to intense police surveillance in England but also to the severe measures taken at home against the IRA by the Fianna Fáil government which was determined that Ireland should not be used as a base for attacks on Britain. After the Anglo-Irish agreements and the 1938 election triumph, de Valera was in a very strong position in dealing with republican extremists. The break between Fianna Fáil and the IRA was now irrevocable. The Offences Against the State Act was passed in June 1939: this provided for the reintroduction of the Military Tribunal and the internment of prisoners without trial. The Treason Act provided the death penalty for acts of treason. In early January 1940 the Emergency Powers Act, under which the Curragh internment camp was opened for IRA detainees, became law, while in Northern Ireland hundreds of IRA supporters were also locked up.

The period from 1940 to 1944 holds perhaps the harshest memories for republican activists. These years saw shootings, executions and deaths from hunger strike as well as internment at the Curragh Camp and many imprisonments. The total of those who died was relatively small but they became republican martyrs: henceforth the IRA regarded Fianna Fáil and the Special Branch with implacable hostility. By the mid-1940s the IRA had apparently been reduced to a small and ineffective group, defeated by state coercion, superior strategy and intelligence, internal dissension and futile wartime intrigue.

5 Neutrality and after, 1939-48

Neutrality in a world conflict is the ultimate exercise in national sovereignty. Apart from the dismantling of the Treaty, a pattern of independent behaviour in the international arena had emerged in the 1920s and 1930s, as had a small state's concern for international peace and order in an anarchic world where power-blocs pursued their own interests. In 1923 Ireland had joined the League of Nations and later sought membership of the League Council where she eventually found admittance in 1930. In 1932 de Valera was elected President of the Council. In a forthright speech he warned the League that force must be repudiated in international politics, and asserted that no state should be permitted to act contrary to the Covenant of the League which was a solemn pact. But de Valera's integrity, statesmanship and common sense found expression in more than words. In 1934, ignoring the possibility of adverse reaction at home, he urged consideration of the question of admitting the Soviet Union into the League of Nations, pointing out the dangers to world peace of the continued exclusion of such an important power. It was a similar sense of correctness and integrity which made him support the League's attitude of non-intervention in the Spanish Civil War, despite the near-hysterical pro-Franco fervour among clericalists in the Irish Free State. Similarly, and again at the risk of domestic unpopularity, the Irish government supported the application of sanctions against Italy in 1935 for its aggression against Ethiopia. For de Valera another guiding principle was that 'small states must not become the tools of any great powers'. From all this it seems clear that, other factors apart, a climate of independence had been established in Irish approaches to international affairs long before 1939.

The good relations established with Britain by the London agreements of 1938 were threatened by the possibility of a crisis over the extension of conscription to Northern Ireland, an issue arousing violent nationalist reaction. Happily a crisis was averted when the British government decided in May 1939 that Northern Ireland would, after all, be excluded from the terms of a military conscription bill.

From early 1939 Ireland was more and more concerned with her position in the coming European conflict. In spite of the return of the ports, many Irishmen doubted whether neutrality was a feasible policy, but the *intention* to stay neutral was clearly stated. De Valera expressed it as the government's aim in a broadcast in February 1939 and again in the Dáil in the following May: 'we believe that no other position would be accepted by the majority of our people as long as the present position (partition) exists'.

On 31 August 1939 de Valera pointed out to Dr Edouard Hempel, the German Minister in Dublin, that although Ireland desired peace with all nations including Germany, the government would have to show a certain consideration for Britain because of geographical and economic considerations. When Germany invaded Poland the following day, the Dáil and Senate were immediately convened. The Dáil enacted, without a division, legislation affirming Ireland's neutrality for the duration of the conflict. The government was given widespread power in the matter of regulating supplies, price control and censorship. There thus began what was quaintly termed 'the emergency'.

There was a divergence of views on neutrality within the ranks of the main opposition party. Fine Gael, after all, had traditionally stood for a policy of close association with the British Commonwealth. Nevertheless, the party as a whole backed neutrality; indeed it expelled its deputy leader, James Dillon, in 1942 for his public and morally courageous repudiation of the national policy.

Partition was the ostensible pretext for Irish neutrality, though ironically the availability of the Northern ports to Britain was one of the main reasons why Irish neutrality was not infringed. But it is ridiculous to suppose that a sense of grievance over partition was the major reason for Irish popular support for neutrality. Rather, there was a universal view that a small state would suffer considerably by voluntarily participating in a war not of its own making. Formal participation in the war on Britain's side, even if backed by a majority of the people, would have created serious internal dissensions: an Irish war effort, in these circumstances, would almost certainly have invited sabotage from extremists. There were divided opinions on the relative merits of the belligerents—there was a strong vein of admiration for Hitler as the architect of his country's reconstruction, and some understandable satisfaction at British setbacks without any real desire to see Britain defeated—but there was near-unanimity that Ireland should not get involved. The evil nature of Nazism was by no means evident to Irishmen in 1939. Above all, neutrality was sensed as the acid test of real independence and what saw it through to eventual success was, in the first place, a remarkable consensus of popular determination.

It is true that volunteer service by many Irishmen in the British forces, for whatever motive, was a welcome contribution to the Allied war effort. Yet the forms of neutrality were scrupulously observed by de Valera, and the recent publication of British government records reveals the very considerable pressure to which he was subjected, first from the British and later from the Americans, on matters ranging from alleged espionage connected with the German and Japanese missions in Dublin to the provision of naval and air bases in the south and west of Ireland. We now know how insistent Churchill was, as First Lord of the Admiralty, that the southern ports should be seized. De Valera was lured with the bait of Irish unity but he rightly rejected this as a promise highly unlikely to be fulfilled. British strategy, aimed at restricting food imports in the hope of causing popular resentment to force de Valera to provide naval facilities, was based on a fallacy since neutrality was not a de Valera-imposed policy as some of Churchill's advisers seemed to imagine.

During the first nine months of the war the pursuit of neutrality did not present any great difficulties but the situation changed radically with the fall of France and the presence of German troops along the north-western shores of Europe. Well before that, however, the British government made strong approaches for naval facilities at Berehaven. From an early stage, the German U-boats were benefiting from the inability of British escort craft and flying boats to cover from English bases a sufficient sea area in the western approaches. But when Sir John Maffey, the U.K. representative in Dublin, approached de Valera on the matter he found the Taoiseach adamant. As Maffey reported: 'The question of the ports was the very nerve centre of public interest in that matter and the public mood would react with intense violence to any action invalidating their integrity.' Maffey's shrewd reading of the situation was a not inconsiderable factor in maintaining tolerable Anglo-Irish relations and continuing, if grudging, respect for Irish neutrality. Thus, though Winston Churchill, then first Lord of the Admiralty, urged that the constitutional position of Irish neutrality should be challenged, the British cabinet as a whole agreed to take the matter no further at that stage.

If the Irish government was indebted to Maffey's sensitive diplomacy, it was no less fortunate in having Edouard Hempel as German Minister in Dublin. He, too, represented to his government the sincerity and determination of the Irish wish for neutrality and he was particularly anxious to avoid any German-IRA intrigues which would give Britain a pretext for intervention. Hempel was of course aware that de Valera's personal sympathy was with the Allies and that Irish neutrality was weighted on the Allied side—British airmen who came down on Irish soil were sent home while their German counterparts were interned—but he did not believe such breaches of impartiality warranted German retaliation.

Irish public feeling took a turn against Germany after the invasion of Belgium and Holland, de Valera protesting 'against the cruel wrong that has been done them'. At the same time the government had to face a very formidable opponent of neutrality in Churchill who had replaced Chamberlain as British premier. About this time also, an all-party consultative defence council was set up and its existence testified to national solidarity. Old Civil War enemies sat on the same platform, as a recruiting drive was launched for the army and auxiliary forces. In May 1940 the military establishment comprised a regular force of 14,000 and a reserve of 12,000. The new drive was a spectacular success and it was later optimistically estimated that in the event of invasion the government could muster an aggregate strength of 250,000 men. Pro-British as well as IRA elements, not to speak of the ubiquitous native begrudgers, might sneer at this ill-trained and poorly-equipped volunteer army as 'chocolate soldiers'; nevertheless their numbers and their enthusiasm gave impressive witness to the popular commitment.

The whole economy was deeply affected by wartime conditions. Perhaps it was not anticipated that German victories would so quickly pose a threat to supplies, the maintenance of which was Ireland's principal economic concern from the summer of 1940. Seán Lemass was the obvious choice to head a new Department of Supplies. Keeping things going rather than making progress became the economic keynote of the war years. Many raw materials were almost completely cut off and there was a heavy fall in industrial production and employment. Emigration to Great Britain rose steadily as the stream to America dried up. As many as 50,000 Irishmen had served with the British forces by the end of the war, and legions of Irish workers poured into British munition factories, hospitals and other areas. British politicians and civil servants were very well aware that in spite of, or perhaps because of, Irish neutrality, Irish labour was making a considerable contribution to the British war effort.

At home the 'emergency' gave a fresh impetus to the

government policy of wheat-growing, and compulsory tillage orders doubled the area under crops during the war years. But those who hoped that agriculture would experience a boom similar to that of World War I were to be disappointed. Farmers had not had the opportunity to recover from the depression of the 1930s, an outbreak of foot-and-mouth disease in 1941 greatly reduced cattle stocks, and British prices for farm products remained low. Supplies of fertilisers and feeding-stocks dwindled and soil fertility was affected. The value of exports was low, and imports were few since finished goods and raw materials were simply not available. In a stagnant wartime economy costs rose as the standard of living fell, and the government pegged down wages and salaries to avoid inflation.

Rationing was the essential method of alleviating the worst consequences of scarcity. Sugar, tea and fuel were rationed at an early stage, clothing and bread followed in 1942, gas and electricity were in short supply while petrol for private motoring ceased in 1942. Coal was replaced by native peat resources, though the quality of much of the peat, or 'turf', remained poor. The railway system was severely affected. Machinery of all kinds proved difficult to maintain under wartime conditions, becoming overworked and obsolete. The period of scarcity and shortages did not end when hostilities ceased in 1945 but continued for at least two years thereafter. One important achievement, however, was the setting up of a state shipping service to provide a minimum supply of essential imports after British ships ceased carrying cargoes to Irish ports in 1942. More generally there was the psychological satisfaction gained from the knowledge that a severe test was being met adequately.

In the summer of 1940 as the Germans advanced westwards, German interest in Ireland not surprisingly became active, though it was never well-informed. It was hoped, apparently, that the IRA would create sufficient diversionary action in Northern Ireland to draw off British troops in other theatres of war. The Irish capture of the German agent, Captain Hermann Goertz, put paid to any real danger of effective German espionage or of a German link-up with the IRA. De Valera was adamant throughout that the country must not be used as a base for any attack on English security. Hempel for his part guaranteed that under no circumstances would the Germans invade Ireland, but also indicated, on instructions from Berlin, that a German victory would mean the end of partition. The government was unlikely to be drawn by this feeler any more than by Churchill's bait of Irish unity. The truth is that neither threat nor promise could reverse the neutrality policy at this stage. The Taoiseach also resisted pressure from David Gray, the American Minister, who strongly held the view that the British should be given the use of the ports – despite the fact that his own country was not yet in the war.

From the time Hitler invaded Russia in June 1941 there was no longer any danger of a German infringement of Irish neutrality. Henceforward whatever threats there were came from the Allies. In December 1941 came the American entry into the war with the Japanese attack on Pearl Harbour. It was the occasion of a characteristically melodramatic telegram from Churchill to de Valera: 'Now or never. "A Nation Once Again". Am very ready to meet you at any time'. The evocative middle phrase was not, it now appears from a recent clarification, a flamboyant promise of unity in return for the abandonment of neutrality but rather an emotional appeal to Ireland to recover its soul by taking the side of the angels. In any case, it was treated by de Valera as rhetorical flourish. The Taoiseach reacted to the American entry by reiterating Ireland's traditional friendship and sympathy with the United States but he repeated that 'the policy of the state remains unchanged'. Nevertheless pressure was kept up by the United States. Roosevelt had little sympathy with the Irish policy and he was strongly influenced by the advice of David Gray who was hostile to de Valera. When American troops were first based in Northern Ireland, de Valera protested against their presence and once again asserted Ireland's right to unity. Despite these tensions, however, the friendly bias of

Irish neutrality persisted and there continued that liaison between British and Irish military chiefs which had begun when a German invasion was feared.

A real sense of crisis developed in February 1944 when both the American and British ministers demanded the removal of German and Japanese diplomats from Dublin on the grounds that they were being provided with 'the opportunity for highly organised espionage'. The 'American note' as it was popularly and correctly called (for the final danger to neutrality appeared to emanate from the American rather than the British side), ignored the fact that a radio transmitter in the German legation had long since been removed at the request of the government. In reply to the note, the Taoiseach claimed that his government had handled espionage attempts successfully and once more he asserted Ireland's right to neutrality. The whole episode further increased de Valera's prestige at home and was an important factor in his election victory in 1944.

The protocol of neutrality was observed by the Taoiseach to the very end, to an extent indeed that his Anglo-American critics regarded as perverse. On the news of Hitler's death, he paid a formal call of condolence on the German Minister, an action which the Allied governments found outrageous.

On 13 May 1945 Churchill broadcast a victory speech which contained a sharp attack on de Valera: 'Had it been necessary we should have been forced to come to close quarters with Mr de Valera. . . . With a restraint and poise to which, I venture to say, history will find few parallels, His Majesty's Government never laid a violent hand upon them, though at times it would have been quite easy and quite natural, and we left the de Valera government to frolic with the German and later with the Japanese representatives to their hearts' content.' Three days later, in the course of a broadcast thanking all those who helped to make neutrality a success and warning of further perils ahead, de Valera made a memorable reply. 'Mr Churchill makes it clear', he said, 'that in certain circumstances he would have violated our neutrality and that he would justify his action by Britain's necessity. It seems strange to me that Mr Churchill does not see that this, if it be accepted, would mean that Britain's necessity would become a moral code. . . . It is indeed hard for the strong to be just to the weak. But acting justly always has its rewards. By resisting his temptation in this instance, Mr Churchill instead of adding another horrid chapter to the already bloodstained record of the relations between England and this country, has advanced the cause of international morality an important step. . . .' Referring to Churchill's expressed pride in Britain's lone stand after France had fallen, the Taoiseach struck an emotional chord in his Irish listeners: 'Could he not find in his heart the generosity to acknowledge that there is a small nation that stood alone not for one year or two, but for several hundred years against aggression?' It was a notable speech: sincere, reasoned, ironical, chiding, magisterial and statesmanlike. It made both an immediate and lasting impression on those who heard it. De Valera had spoken for all the people he had led during the war years: it was, arguably, his finest hour.

More than any other event since independence, neutrality put a stamp on the state and underlined its homogeneity. The success of the policy not only saved the country from the ravages of war, it did much to emphasise the consciousness of sovereignty, renew a sense of national confidence, heal the wounds of the Civil War through a common dedication to a national purpose and at the same time, paradoxically, sublimate anti-British hostility. The success and popularity of neutrality laid the basis for the development of an independent foreign policy at a later date. But there was a heavy debit side. The economy ticked over at a subsistence level and continued to stagnate in the postwar years. Indeed, stagnation embraced the whole sphere of politics and society. The Fianna Fáil government's continued tenure of office was mainly due to its achievements in directing neutrality. Emigration drained off potential malcontents and the conservation of a rural homogeneous insular society was deepened by wartime isolation. Life in Ireland during the 'emergency' years was static and dull: the cultural and intellectual impoverishment of the previous decades was intensified. Above all, Twenty-Six County neutrality and Six-County involvement further widened the gulf which had long since yawned between nationalist Ireland and the Northern Unionists.

It now becomes necessary to examine the political scene during the 'emergency' period. After the adoption of neutrality the political party system continued to function but there were suggestions from time to time – though not by Fianna Fáil – that it should be set aside and a national government formed. This was never done because in the last analysis de Valera would not have it, secure in his comfortable majority for most of the period and confident that he and his party team could deal with the various. problems presented by the war. In any case, there was never from 1939 to 1945 a national crisis of a really acute nature.

However, the war years witnessed a diminution of intensity in party politics: not until the 1948 election was there something like a return to the excitement of the 1930s. Political tempers had cooled and the gap between Fianna Fáil and Fine Gael political and economic policies was being considerably narrowed. The whole tempo of political life was slowed down by wartime conditions. National security demanded some form of party truce which was effective in the sphere of defence. Representatives of all parties sat on the Defence Council and appeared together on recruiting platforms, and time given to the Red Cross or the local security forces meant some neglect of the affairs of the political branch. Party organisation was thus impaired by 'emergency' conditions and party publicity at election times was affected by the restrictions on travel and newsprint. But the slackening in political activity was less detrimental, in the nature of things, to the party in office than to its political opponents.

By 1938 there could already be detected in the Fianna

Fáil party some elements of change. It was a tribute to the effectiveness of the party's propaganda that while managing to give the impression of being *the* party of the underprivileged, it greatly widened its base of support. It was becoming a party of an irreproachably respectable dye and was beginning to attract the men of property and position who had originally attached themselves to the pro-Treaty side and who had been dismayed by the advent of de Valera to power in 1932. Fianna Fáil's industrial protectionist policy had involved it with the world of business and the pressure of businessmen in the party helped to modify its initially radical, or at least populist, policies as set out in its official aims. In office, the party found itself using the repressive apparatus of state power in dealing with republican extremists and this also tended to change its political complexion. Inevitably, it found patronage at its disposal, the result not only of its years in office and of its state-wide organisation but of its penetration of local government; it had long since grasped the importance of control in this sphere. Increasingly, many people were bound, or felt themselves to be bound, to the party by self-interest no less than by conviction.

The religious minority came to appreciate a government which was no longer militantly republican or irredentist, had no socialist designs on Protestant commercial wealth, did not seem to be as closely identified with the Catholic middle class as its main opponents – though in reality it was just as susceptible to clericalist pressures – a government which, above all, had demonstrated its capacity to govern, dealing firmly with threats from right and left.

The policy of neutrality was backed by all parties but most redounded to the credit of Fianna Fáil and was effectively exploited to party advantage in the war-time elections. The message conveyed to the people was that only de Valera's achievements had made neutrality feasible in the first place and only his leadership would see the country safely through the war. 'Don't change horses when crossing the stream' was the Fianna Fáil slogan in the 1943 campaign: by implication, at least, the sincerity and competence of

Fine Gael in respect of neutrality were being questioned. In the economic sphere, there was reasonable satisfaction with Lemass's maintenance of supplies: it was a shrewd piece of political psychology to prepare the public for the worst when the worst never came. It also suited the government that the various exigencies of the 'emergency' period necessarily limited the activities of the opposition: indeed, opposition beyond a certain limit could always be branded as a danger to national solidarity and security.

The period from 1937 to 1948 was one of disastrous decline for Fine Gael. All the cards seemed stacked against the party. Its association with the quasi-fascist Blueshirt movement had badly damaged its prestige and long after it had returned to its orthodox parliamentary role the traumatic experience continued to haunt it – and its political opponents made sure that it would not be forgotten. The failure of the party to restore its lost fortunes in the 1937 election was significant: the reasonably favourable circumstances then prevailing, after four and a half years of controversial Fianna Fáil rule, were destined not to be repeated. De Valera's successful negotiation of the 1938 Anglo-Irish agreements was a bad blow to Fine Gael.

The outbreak of the war raised a serious dilemma for a party with a Commonwealth commitment. It was acutely aware that to support neutrality was virtually to abandon its Commonwealth position and to lose one of its few distinguishing marks while to oppose neutrality would have been futile as well as highly unpopular. In the event it supported the national policy faithfully, even to the extent of expelling its deputy leader, James Dillon. Yet some suspicion persisted about the party's real feelings, and this was hardly allayed by Richard Mulcahy's advocacy in 1944 of an Anglo-Irish military alliance as a future plank in the party's platform. In a period of revived nationalist sentiment the imputation of 'West British' leanings was damaging. Another factor which militated against popular support for Fine Gael was the aura of middle-class respectability which clung to the party and this, ironically, at a time when it was already losing middle-class votes to Fianna Fáil.

In the 1943 election it suffered a calamitous loss of 13 seats and thereafter began to wear a tired air of resignation. It became characterised by the backward look, a party in seemingly permanent opposition which had lost the will to govern. A further setback was the retirement of W. T. Cosgrave from the leadership in January 1944. Tired and unwell, he regarded Fine Gael's future as problematical and felt that his leadership could help it no further. With his departure from the front bench there died the interest of those who had remained in active politics out of affection and respect for Cosgrave. It added to the impression of the party's weakness that its new leader, Richard Mulcahy, was at that time without a seat in the Dáil. In 1948 its share of the popular vote fell below 20 per cent and the political pundits could be forgiven for thinking its extinction imminent: in fact, the sick man of Irish politics was to make a miraculous recovery.

Numerous factors account for the weakness of the Labour Party in the years after independence, a weakness at first sight surprising in a society of poverty, unemployment and bad housing conditions. It is arguable that it never really recovered from its decision not to contest the 1918 general election. At a time when the franchise was greatly extended and a whole new generation was being politicised, the electorate was deprived of the opportunity of forming a Labour-voting habit. Though the party performed a valuable service to parliamentary democracy by constituting the opposition in the Dáil before Fianna Fáil's entry, the polarisation of Irish politics around the Treaty and the prevailing obsession with constitutional issues continued to relegate Labour to the background. Other adverse factors were the lack of support from a rural society largely composed of conservative small farmer-owners; the draining off by emigration of social discontent and therefore of potential support for Labour; the absence both of an industrial proletariat (there were as many domestic servants –

85,000 – as factory workers in 1926) and of a numerically significant agricultural labouring class; and the gulf between the northern and southern working classes sealed by partition. Labour's appeal was narrowly and basically 'manual' working class and not until the 1960s did it even *try* to attract a wider social support, or appeal to intellectuals.

The parliamentary Labour Party gave the impression of a group whose main purpose seemed to be the defence or promotion of trades union interests in the Dáil; paradoxically the general body of trade unionists did not give their electoral allegiance to Labour. In the rural areas there was little sense of a national party with declared general objectives: rural Labour was rather a series of electoral committees, each deputy being the leader of his own party, as it were, respected by his constituents for his public service and his apparent skill in redressing their grievances. The party was identified in the public mind entirely with the poorer classes and thus suffered the consequences of Irish rural and small-town petty snobbery. Few professional men, even if they had been actively wooed by the party, would have cared to join Labour. Similarly, the farmer was not attracted by a party which commanded the allegiance of his labouring men.

If Labour had unequivocally adopted Connolly's robust socialism it might have won considerably more industrial and urban support, as well as that of some intellectuals. On the other hand, in the repressive climate of the period, socialism was a taboo concept, frequently and deliberately blurred with Communism, and politically dangerous to expound. Periodic red scares and smears did more harm to Labour than to any other group. When the party boldly adopted a real socialist programme in 1936, including nationalisation of all basic industries and state control of banking, displeasure was later expressed by the Catholic hierarchy. As a result, the phrase 'Workers' Republic' was abandoned and the nationalisation clauses considerably diluted. Indeed, there was opposition to the socialist programme from within the Labour Party itself.

But perhaps the most important reason for Labour's chronically weak position was simply this: it could not seriously compete with Fianna Fáil for the support of working-class voters. Its 'natural' voters, rural and urban, were lured away by the Fianna Fáil blend of populist reform and nationalism under de Valera's leadership. Indeed Fianna Fáil was making the infuriating claim that *it* was the Labour party. With its reformist policies pre-empted, Labour did not even have the real alternative of espousing socialism. 'Extremists' and 'idealists' saw Labour as unappealing and sought a more congenial climate in the IRA or in left-wing fringe organisations.

However, Labour experienced a resurgence in the early 1940s as organisation improved and new branches were formed. It performed impressively in the local government elections of 1942, particularly in Dublin, a barometer of the strength or weakness of radicalism in Irish politics. In the 1943 general election it increased its Dáil strength from 9 to 17, benefiting, again notably in Dublin, from the public reaction to the pinch of the war-time economy, from the discontent with rationing, higher prices, static wages, industrial unemployment, increased emigration and, more generally, from popular disenchantment with a government which had already lost its initial radical momentum. When, however, Fianna Fáil formed a minority government Labour abstained in the re-election of de Valera as Taoiseach.

The favourable indications for Labour in 1943 were reversed by a bitter crisis within the party the following year against a background of inter-union hostility. In origin, the trouble went back to 1923-24 and the ousting of the turbulent Jim Larkin from the historic trade union which he had founded in 1908 – the Irish Transport and General Workers' Union. During his absence in America from 1914 to 1923 the ITGWU grew in strength under the direction of Thomas Foran and William O'Brien who were determined not to relinquish control to Larkin on his return. The Workers' Union of Ireland was founded in June 1924 as a breakaway Larkinite organisation but

O'Brien saw to it that the WUI continued to be excluded from the Irish Trades Union Congress. The quarrel not only damaged trade union effectiveness over a long period but contributed to the weakness of Labour as a political force. It was not of course entirely a clash between strong personalities but also a direct conflict of two concepts of trade unionism. Larkin believed that a union should be used as an instrument in the destruction of capitalist society: O'Brien saw trade unions as the means of improving the workers' lot within the status quo. It was the immemorial difference among socialists between revolution and reformism.

Larkin's opposition to government measures in 1941 (favouring the more powerful unions, particularly the ITGWU) brought him back to active politics. In 1943 he won one of four Labour seats in Dublin despite a planned red scare. O'Brien and the ITGWU had tried to prevent Larkin being nominated as a Dáil candidate and the old feud flared up again. When an attempt to expel Larkin from the Labour Party failed, the ITGWU, the largest union in Ireland, took the drastic step of disaffiliating from the Labour Party. The financial loss thus involved was serious enough for Labour but worse was to come. Of the eight ITGWU members among the Labour T.D.s, five seceded to form the National Labour Party: there followed allegations by the breakaway group and by the ITGWU that the Communists had infiltrated the Labour Party, especially in Dublin. The bitter split prevented Labour from consolidating its 1943 gains and from making a sporting bid for power in the more flexible post-war political atmosphere. In the 1944 election, the split cost the Labour movement as a whole a total loss of five seats. Labour representation was now reduced to 12 (8 Labour, 4 National Labour) and Larkin lost his seat. The participation of both groups in the 1948 coalition paved the way for political reunion in 1950. However there was no such reconciliation in the trade union movement: in 1945 the ITGWU and other Irish-based unions broke with the Irish TUC and set up the Congress of Irish Trade Unions based on the notion that Irish workers must not be dominated by British-based unions. Larkin's WUI was, of course, in the TUC camp. Not until 1959 did labour solidarity finally triumph over political squabbling and chauvinistic sensibilities, when a reunited Irish Congress of Trade Unions ended a long dispute which had been so costly to the interests of organised labour. It was much later before the trade unions contributed in any significant fashion to Labour finances.

In the lacklustre election campaign of 1943, a new farmers' party made an impressive début. For many years there had been no separate political representation of the farming interest. In 1938, a new farmers' party, Clann na Talmhan ('Children of the Land') was founded. It grew out of dissatisfaction with lack of farming progress under Fianna Fáil and with the general neglect of the West, and later thrived on the disappointing realisation that the agricultural boom of the Great War was not now being repeated. It differed from earlier farmers' parties in that its appeal was primarily to the small farmers of the West rather than to large farming or ranching interests. Its objectives included reduced rating, land reclamation and increased afforestation. It was confronted by the classic problems facing Irish political farming organisations – the difficulty of accommodating the diverse interests of farmers engaged in different types and scales of farming; the lack of cohesion between different regions, including difficulties in travel and communications; above all, perhaps, the blurring of political lines resulting from the presence of farmers in other parties with agricultural policies of their own. Nevertheless, Clann na Talmhan flourished in the early war years, drawing sustenance from farming discontent with the static agricultural prices of the 'emergency' economy. The party overcame the difficulties of wartime campaigning to win 10 seats in the 1943 election and at least four other T.D.s independently represented farming interests. Its performance in the Dáil was never impressive. Its members were political innocents abroad; they never rose above sectional aims, and made no attempt to expand the party outside the south and west. Their Dáil strength declined slowly in 1944 and 1948, but in the latter year their seven seats were important in forming the first inter-party government. Thereafter the party maintained only a formal existence. Though the achievements of Clann na Talmhan were not negligible, its history showed, not for the first time, that even at a period when the economy was predominantly agricultural a party concerned with promoting exclusively agricultural policies could not hope to win sustained substantial support from the rural community itself, let alone the electorate at large.

Towards the end of the war the Fianna Fáil position looked unassailable. De Valera had restored his 1943 losses and had regained a strong overall majority in May 1944 in the second wartime election, a 'snap' campaign characteristically exploiting all the advantages – the renewed threat to neutrality of the 'American note' episode, the Labour split and the further upset to Fine Gael caused by Cosgrave's retirement. Fianna Fáil strength was further demonstrated in 1945 by the victory of the party's candidate for the Presidency, Seán T. Ó Ceallaigh (538,000 votes) over his opponents, Fine Gael's Seán MacEoin (335,000) and Patrick MacCartan, an Independent of republican background (200,000). However, MacCartan's impressive showing as a third-party candidate, particularly in Dublin, indicated that there was a substantial anti-Fianna Fáil vote not prepared to help revive the moribund Fine Gael party.

The object of the government after the war was to achieve economic recovery as quickly as possible. Before the end of 1945 a beginning was made with building programmes and rural electrification. Yet the country continued to experience the restrictions and shortages of the wartime economy. The very wet summer of 1946 had an adverse effect on grain production and in 1947 bread rationing had to be introduced. The severe winter of 1947 was aggravated by a fuel crisis which reacted on industry and transport. As prices rose and imports increased, wages were still pegged down and exports decreased. In autumn

1947 a supplementary budget provided for increased taxation to finance higher food subsidies. Much of the country's economic difficulties were part of a general European pattern but it was natural that public discontent in Ireland should have focussed on the government. Fianna Fáil had been in power without interruption since 1932, and there was a general feeling, typical of post-war moods elsewhere, that it was time for a change. Fianna Fáil, still harping on its neutrality policy accomplishments, seemed to be out of touch with the realities of wages and prices. Discontent with the cost of living found expression in the activities of a militant housewives' association and in a number of bitter strikes, particularly that of the primary teachers who were heavily represented in the new Clann na Poblachta party. Other grievances included the chronic problems of unemployment and emigration, the low level of social services and, in a vague way, the unfulfilled aspiration of Irish unity. Within the Fianna Fáil party itself there was frustration among the younger members as the old guard of the 1916-23 generation continued to dominate the organisation.

It was against this background of boredom, discontent and frustration that we must consider the most interesting political phenomenon of the post-war period – the rapid rise and fall of Clann na Poblachta ('Children of the Republic'). It represented at once the recognition by some republican activists of the futility of their methods and a spectacular attempt to break the moulds of Treaty politics. Its wellspring was the 'republican university'– the jails and internment camps of the 1940s – and its first beginnings were the committees formed to help IRA prisoners. It was formally established in Dublin on 6 July 1946 and its programme had an appeal similar to that of Fianna Fáil in 1932: an attractive blend of radical republicanism (with a fresh emphasis on a united Ireland) and of social and economic reform. It had a ready-made core of support among many republican activists of the 1930s and 1940s and the blessing of some veterans of the 1916-23 period. The party also had a colourful leader in Seán MacBride, son of the executed 1916 man John MacBride and the famous Maud Gonne.

MacBride was a former chief of staff of the IRA, and his family background as well as his own career – particularly his valuable legal work for republican prisoners – made him an almost automatic choice for leadership. The impression of a certain exotic element in his personality was an additional attraction in an Irish political chief.

There was considerable appeal in the party's plea for an end to the residual bitterness of the Civil War and of the 1930s. Members were welcomed irrespective of their past affiliations – 'we don't care what colour shirt you wore.' Paradoxically, then, a movement whose initial impetus was republican attracted people with a pro-Treaty or even a Blueshirt past, as well as Fianna Fáil dissidents. The prospect it held out of efficient, perhaps dynamic, government drew the attention of some young businessmen who were ready to welcome a progressive alternative to Fianna Fáil. Unfortunately, it also attracted many who saw in it simply an expression of their own discontent. The wide political and social spectrum of support was, under stress, to disclose a dangerous divergence of view on the relative importance of nationalist-political issues on the one hand, and socio-economic objectives on the other.

Thoughout 1947 the new party developed rather too rapidly. Only Fianna Fáil had succeeded in the formidable task of building up its organisation in every constituency as Clann na Poblachta now tried to do. The party's trial of strength came before it had time to establish any real cohesion or discipline, but then the timing of the challenge was not of its own choosing. Its success in two (Dublin County; South Tipperary) of three by-elections in November 1947 caused de Valera to decide on an immediate dissolution before the new party could strengthen its position. His decision did not find complete favour with all his followers some of whom believed that the government should have weathered the storm.

The ensuing election of February 1948 was the most exciting since Blueshirt days. The challenge to a jaded government from the young party caught the imagination of the electors at home, and of outside observers. With a panel of 93, Clann had the second largest group of candidates. The mood of the country in 1947, and the results of the by-elections seemed convincing proof at the time that the party was riding on the crest of a wave. Yet the nomination of so many candidates, at least two to every constituency, imposed a severe organisational and financial strain on the resources of a fledgling party. Nevertheless, even those Clann leaders who admitted to misgivings on this score still hoped for a return of at least 20 to 25 candidates while more starry-eyed supporters spoke about a repeat of the 1918 landslide.

From Clann's viewpoint it was a tantalising campaign. The enthusiastic meetings, the processions and bonfires and the acclaim for the party leader recalled the colourful elections of the 1930s. But in the last days before polling MacBride sensed that the tide had turned and that caution and conservatism would, after all, prevent the electors from deserting their traditional party allegiances. Clann's proposals for ending partition, as well as its views on such matters as external relations and the repatriation of sterling assets, were inexpertly propounded from many a Clann platform and were quickly seized on by the party's opponents to discredit it in the electorate's eyes as immature and irresponsible.

In the event, 10 candidates were returned, 6 from the Dublin area. In a number of cases the margin of defeat was exasperatingly small. It could be claimed, of course, that for a young party to win 10 seats at its first attempt was, in the conservative Irish context, a distinct victory: in fact, set against such great expectations, the results were a blow to Clann followers. The comparatively poor performance of the party had one important psychological result in Irish politics: it helped to confirm the conservatism of the electorate and militated against the prospects of other new parties which might be formed in the future.

6 Coalitions versus Fianna Fáil 1948-57

Though the 1948 election returned Fianna Fáil as the largest single party (68 seats out of 147) it lost its overall majority, and the number of first preference votes it received was the lowest at any general election since 1927. Fine Gael's share of the total vote dropped below 20 per cent for the first time but its Dáil strength rose marginally from 30 to 31. An alternative government to Fianna Fáil could be secured only by a coalition of all the other parties and some of the Independents. Clann na Poblachta's decision to participate in the proposed coalition was reached by a very narrow majority at a crucial meeting of the party's national executive. Though the decision alienated the republican rank-and-file, it was a logical one: the great slogan of the election had been 'put them out' and it was now in Clann's power to drive from office an administration whose treatment of republicans had made it more odious, in the eyes of Clann na Poblachta, than Fine Gael whose anti-republican misdeeds lay, after all, in the remoter past. The reluctance of National Labour to participate was also overcome. Finally inter-party agreement was reached on a general ten-point programme between Fine Gael, Clann na Poblachta, Labour, National Labour, Clann na Talmhan and some Independents. The position of Taoiseach and the lion's share of the cabinet posts went to Fine Gael as the largest component. The nominee for Taoiseach was John A. Costello, a distinguished lawyer and former Cumann na nGaedheal attorney general. When the Dáil met, the strength of coalition numbers ensured the election of Costello as Taoiseach, and the ministries in his government were distributed among the various parties in proportion to their Dáil strength. Thus Fine Gael secured the all-important Ministry of Finance (P. McGilligan belonged to the conservative Cumann na nGaedheal tradition in economics), Defence (Dr T. F. O'Higgins of Blueshirt fame), Justice (General Seán MacEoin, a veteran of the Anglo-Irish War) and Industry and Commerce (Daniel Morrissey). The ebullient James Dillon, in temporary exile from Fine Gael, was given Agriculture; the Labour members in government were William Norton (Tánaiste – deputy premier – and Minister for Social Welfare) and T. J. Murphy (Local Government); Posts and Telegraphs went to J. Everett (National Labour) while Lands and Fisheries was entrusted to Joseph Blowick (Clann na Talmhan). Clann na Poblachta supplied two ministers who were to be the centre of explosive controversy – Seán MacBride (External Affairs) and Noel Browne (Health), the latter attaining cabinet rank on his first day as deputy.

Given the diversity of the participating parties, the precarious nature of the coalition's majority over Fianna Fáil, the solidarity of the opposition and the political novelty of the whole experiment, the pundits might be forgiven for predicting a short life for the coalition, yet it lasted three years – the average parliamentary lifespan since independence – and might well have endured longer had it not been for the dramatic nature of the crisis which led to its downfall. The factors which ensured its survival included Costello's skill and patience as chairman, avoidance of legislation likely to alienate any of the constituent elements, a considerable degree of independence in the various ministries and the strong cohesive effect of fear of de Valera's return to power.

The coalition showed that the polarisation of politics around the Civil War was not immutable. There are times in a parliamentary democracy when change even for the sake of change is desirable, and the breaking of Fianna Fáil monopoly was a healthy development. A fresh breeze blew through the corridors of government and civil service. The spell in opposition was a salutary corrective to the staleness and complacency which had overtaken Fianna

Fáil and gave that party an opportunity and incentive to overhaul its organisation. Fine Gael got its first taste of office in sixteen years and regained its self-confidence. It turned to the business of organising itself properly and of interesting youth in its party. Moreover, the continuation of the coalition idea throughout the 1950s brought more benefit to Fine Gael than to any other group, as is evident from its remarkably increased Dáil strength – 31 in 1948 to 40 in 1951 to 50 in 1954. The first coalition brought advantages to Labour also: it gained in terms of responsibility and experience and was enabled to heal its divisions. At the same time, it must be said that William Norton's main preoccupation in office was the maintenance of inter-party cooperation and the continuing existence of the government as a whole rather than the promotion of specifically Labour interests.

The new broom in office showed considerable talent and enthusiasm in grappling with the country's problems. These years saw the beginnings of the policy of state capital investment. The Land Rehabilitation Project was introduced in 1949 and its aim was to use massive state aid to bring back into full production 4 million acres of land which had remained undeveloped because of shortage of capital and technical resources. The scheme was associated with the name of James Dillon, Minister for Agriculture, as was the Anglo-Irish Trade Agreement of 1948 which secured favourable terms for Irish agricultural produce by linking the prices paid for Irish cattle and sheep to the prices received by British farmers. The numbers on the land continued to decrease though there was some progress in the industrial sphere where the Industrial Development Authority was set up, a body which could claim much of the credit for subsequent expansion. In time, Córas Tráchtála was to be equally successful: its function was to promote trade, first with the dollar area and subsequently with the rest of the world. On the other hand, it took a long time before tourism was properly promoted, though its importance as a source of external income was duly recognised. There was considerable progress in housing construction which, after a period of expansion under Fianna Fáil in the 1930s, had been at a standstill during the war years. Under the dynamic direction of Noel Browne in the Department of Health, there was an intensive and successful drive, financed mainly from the Hospitals' Sweepstakes funds, to eradicate tuberculosis which had long been a major health scourge, accounting for 3,000-4,000 deaths per annum in 1948 mainly in the twenty to thirty-four age group. Progress in many of the fields mentioned above would not have been possible without the country's participation (begun by Fianna Fáil) in the European Recovery Programme which provided grants and loans to the extent of about 150 million dollars by 1950. However, there was an obverse side to these first attempts at economic expansion. Inflation had been something of a problem for Fianna Fáil in its last years of power and, aggravated perhaps by capital investment, it was increasingly to trouble the coalition. White-collar workers especially expressed discontent as prices mounted after the Korean war broke out in the summer of 1950. The establishment of the Prices Advisory Board in January 1951 did not solve the problem.

It is worth emphasising at this point that the beginnings of economic planning are to be found in this first coalition period, predating by seven years Dr T. K. Whitaker's famous memo to the Department of Finance in 1956, which is still popularly believed to be the point of departure for government economic programming. As early as January 1949 Ireland's Long Term Recovery Programme was published as a White Paper by the government and set out a consistent set of economic targets and policies for the period 1949 to 1953. The programme was drawn up at the request of the Organisation for European Economic Co-operation (OEEC) as a response to Marshall Aid. Under an agreement signed with the United States government in June 1948 Ireland received an allotment of £47 million worth of Marshall Aid over the next three years. As a condition of this aid the Irish government was required to draw up a programme showing our import requirements over this period. At this time the Department of Finance was apathetic, if not hostile, to the idea of economic programming and it is noteworthy that responsibility for producing the White Paper rested with the Department of External Affairs under Seán MacBride and the department's secretary, F. H. Boland. In contrast to later programmes, it focussed largely on the *external* economic position and only implicitly contained national income projections. The programme emphasised agricultural, particularly livestock, production and asserted that Ireland's special advantages for export surplus lay in livestock and 'not in bread and grain production'. In fact, the Land Rehabilitation Programme, envisaging the investment of £40 million over ten years, was the most important aspect of the whole programme. If the times were out of joint and the Long Term Recovery Programme not an auspicious success, nevertheless it stimulated such important institutional developments as the Central Statistics Office, Córas Tráchtála and the Industrial Development Authority. In any case, it deserves the historian's attention as an Irish government's first exercise in economic planning.

Undoubtedly the most dramatic development of the first coalition was the declaration of a republic. It will be recalled that the External Relations Act of 1936 had created a subtle, if not ambiguous, relationship with Britain and the Commonwealth. This was a characteristic de Valera compromise which his opponents, for various reasons, had continued to criticise. In July 1945 when James Dillon asked in a Dáil question whether or not the state was a republic, Mr de Valera gave a typical reply. 'The state', he said, 'possessed every characteristic mark by which a Republic can be distinguished or recognised.' The External Relations Act, authorising the British king to act in matters regarding the appointment of diplomatic and consular representatives on the advice of the Irish government, was a simple statute repealable at any time, and so 'we are an independent Republic associated as a matter of our external policy with states of the British Commonwealth'. However, Britain and the Dominions took the view that the 1937 Constitution in conjunction with the External Relations

Act had not fundamentally altered Irish relations with the Commonwealth as laid out in the 1921 Treaty. Thus, London and Dublin were interpreting the existing position differently but both appreciated its advantages: on the Irish side the door was still ajar for Irish unity (or so it was fondly believed) and, for the British, the appearance at least of Commonwealth unity was being preserved.

However, among Irish politicians generally, there was a feeling that what was derisively called the 'dictionary republic' was an unsatisfactory and unacceptable constitutional position. The constitutional issue had not been raised during the 1948 election but during the summer of that year, under strong pressure from Labour and, naturally, from Clann na Poblachta, the government decided in favour of repeal of the External Relations Act. Fine Gael, though displeased with the existing constitutional position, had been traditionally in favour of closer association with the Commonwealth. Nevertheless it was the party's earnest hope, particularly that of Costello, that the adoption of a clearcut constitutional position might satisfy republicans and 'take the gun out of politics'. In August 1948, the Tánaiste, William Norton, asserted in the Dáil that 'it would do our national self-respect good both at home and abroad if we were to proceed without delay to abolish the External Relations Act', and de Valera's comment was 'you will get no opposition from us'. It had long since been established that a dominion had the right to secede from the Commonwealth as Sir Stafford Cripps, on behalf of the British cabinet, had explicitly stated at a press conference in New Delhi in 1942.

Nevertheless, there was astonishment when the news broke that a Fine Gael-led government was about to execute a constitutional *volte face*. The timing and the circumstances were completely unexpected. On 1 September 1948, Costello, as a guest of the Canadian Bar Association in Montreal, delivered an address on 'Ireland and International Affairs', the text of which had already been approved by the cabinet before he left Ireland. In it he referred to the 'inaccuracies and infirmities' of the External

Relations Act. Within the next few days the Taoiseach was guest at official dinners in Montreal and Ottawa where the toast of 'The King' to the exclusion of 'The President of Ireland' was proposed. This illustrated the 'inaccuracies and infirmities' of the Irish constitutional position. On 5 September the *Sunday Independent* carried the headline 'External Relations Act to go' and the Taoiseach at a press conference in Ottawa two days later confirmed that this indeed was the government's intention. To a correspondent who enquired whether this meant secession from the Commonwealth, the Taoiseach replied in the affirmative. The news caused quite a stir in Ireland and though we now know that the Taoiseach was giving expression to a cabinet decision already taken, there appeared to be grounds at the time for thinking that a crucially important constitutional decision had been made in an arbitrary fashion several thousand miles away. Many were astonished that the announcement had been made without any regard for diplomatic protocol and were no less amazed at a Fine Gael change of policy which had not been aired at the general election seven months before. Not surprisingly, Fianna Fáil deputies were particularly critical.

In November 1948 the flamboyantly-styled Republic of Ireland Bill was introduced in the Dáil. Its purpose, as stated in the preamble, was to repeal the External Relations Act, to declare that the description of the state should be the Republic of Ireland and to enable the President to exercise executive powers or functions in connection with the state's external relations. The Taoiseach hoped it would end bitterness in Irish politics and improve rather than worsen relations with Britain and the Commonwealth. Fianna Fáil deputies felt that the Bill would make the ending of partition more difficult: nevertheless, they gave it their support though de Valera had to use persuasion to prevent some of them from voting against it. The Republic of Ireland Act came into force on Easter Monday 1949.

The British Prime Minister, Clement Atlee, complained that he had been given no notice of the Irish government's intentions, but relations with Britain remained smooth while the implications of the Irish action were considered. Both Britain and the Republic safeguarded by legislation the rights of Irish citizens and British subjects in each other's countries. Existing trade preferences were maintained. In the British view it was felt more advantageous that the Irish should remain a 'non-foreign' people, continuing to have the same status in Britain as subjects of the United Kingdom. (Irish affairs would continue to be dealt with by the Commonwealth Relations Office, not by the Foreign Office.) In coming to this decision (a welcome one for the mass of Irishmen, especially those in Britain), the British government was in part influenced by the views of representatives of the Canadian, Australian and New Zealand governments that the Irish action should not be allowed to impair relations between Ireland and Commonwealth countries.

The impact of the Republic of Ireland Act on Northern Ireland was immediate. Once again, as at the time of the Anglo-Irish negotiations in 1938, the Ulster Unionists proclaimed that the province was in danger and called for a rally of Unionist opinion. In the 1949 general election in Northern Ireland, there was a predictable accession of strength to the government on the constitutional issue. Though funds from an anti-partition drive in the South supported anti-partition candidates, the Unionists won four extra seats and Northern Ireland Labour, whose acceptance of partition in a bid to attract Protestant workers only alienated its Catholic supporters, lost all its representation at Stormont. But the Unionists had even more cause for satisfaction. They secured from the British Labour Government the reassurances of the Ireland Act of 1949 which declared that 'the part of Ireland heretofore known as Éire ceased as from the eighteenth day of April 1949 to be part of His Majesty's dominions' and went on to give a solemn guarantee that 'in no event will Northern Ireland or any part thereof cease to be a part of His Majesty's dominions and of the United Kingdom without the consent of the parliament of Northern Ireland'. Here the imperial parliament – and a Labour-dominated one, at that – seemed to be renouncing its own absolute right to dispose of Northern Ireland. To the Unionists, the Act appeared to be a permanent guarantee of their ascendancy: in fact, its air of permanence turned out to be as illusory as that attending the Act of Union itself. In the Republic, the Ireland Act was seen as slamming the door on Irish unity and the reaction was a great deal of sound and fury. As had happened before, anti-partition noises from the South simply served to ensure the solidarity of Northern Unionists.

It was a cherished hope of those who declared the Republic that extremist sentiment would be thereby appeased and violence in Irish politics diminished, if not ended. Already the coalition government had released several republican prisoners in the hope of 'taking the gun out of politics', but it was a hope that soon proved to be premature. In the political theology of republicans, acceptance of the Free State and its institutions was a betrayal of the mystical republic: no amount of subsequent tinkering was acceptable to 'legitimists' who looked back to the Second Dáil as the only true republican parliament. Indeed, the early 1950s saw the beginnings of Sinn Féin reorganisation which preceded an IRA resurgence. The public outcry against partition, the Ireland Act and the futility of the constitutional anti-partition campaign helped to bring in new republican recruits. Because of the delicate balance of the elements in the coalition government no steps were taken to prevent illegal organisations from holding public meetings.

In retrospect, it would appear at first sight that the declaration of the Republic was unnecessary, precipitate and fruitless – entrenching the Northern Unionists in their position, destroying a possible bridge to unity, leaving the gun in politics and involving a futile and frustrating anti-partition campaign. Moreover, in the same year in which Ireland seceded from the Commonwealth, India as a Republic remained a member, influenced, ironically, by what had been the Irish invention of external association.

It was not to be the only country to demonstrate that republican status was compatible with Commonwealth membership. But perhaps republican status had a very different significance for the two countries. In the case of Ireland, the decision to adopt such a status was bound up with the intangible, though none the less real, factor of national honour and self-respect, heightened perhaps by the experience of neutrality. In the last analysis, Ireland's very closeness to Britain and the past relationship between the two countries made Irishmen feel that even the most shadowy constitutional connection suggested a position of subordination and made an adoption of formal sovereignty imperative, whatever the consequences. One consequence, at least, was to emphasise how divergent were the developments of both parts of Ireland since 1922. The Republic of Ireland Act embodied one aspiration of a homogeneous, nationalist state: to say the least, it made no attempt to reconcile that aspiration with the cherished one of territorial unity.

The immediate post-war period also witnessed the tentative resumption of Ireland's contacts with the larger world, as she emerged from the insularity of the emergency years. The first public indication of Irish interest in the recently-founded United Nations Organisation came in July 1946 when the then Taoiseach, Éamon de Valera, tabled a motion in the Dáil expressing Irish agreement with the principles of the Charter and recommending Irish membership. However, the Soviet Union used its power of veto to exclude Ireland, an exclusion which was to last until 1955 when she was admitted as part of a package deal between East and West by which new members from one bloc were balanced by those from the other. Yet, during her nine years of exclusion, Ireland played some part in the activities of some of the UN specialised agencies – the Food and Agricultural Organisation, for example.

Governments in post-war Europe were preoccupied with two main concerns – the establishment of Western military strength against what was seen as Communist aggression, and the business of economic recovery, which was also regarded as a bulwark against Communism. Ireland felt unable to participate in military alliances and did not adhere to the five-power Brussels Treaty of March 1948 or to the North Atlantic Treaty Organisation of April 1949. 'Our sympathies lie clearly with Western Europe', said Seán MacBride in July 1948 and this reflected the views of different Irish governments as did MacBride's qualification – 'the continuance of partition precludes us from taking our rightful place in the affairs of Europe'. In a memorandum drawn up in response to an invitation to become a member of NATO in 1949, the government stated that while in agreement with the general aim of the Treaty, Ireland could not adhere to the organisation because of the fact that British forces occupied six Irish counties. (The significant point here was that NATO guaranteed the territorial integrity of its member states.) While partition lasted, the Irish memorandum declared, any Anglo-Irish alliance would incur the risk of civil war in Ireland itself. North Atlantic security would be best served by the ending of partition 'which threatened the peace of these islands'. As the 1950s wore on, a growing number of Irish people approved of non-adherence to NATO because, leaving aside the partition issue, the attitude was seen as a continuation of the neutrality policy and as the adoption of an independent stance in international affairs.

While rejecting membership of NATO, Ireland had no reservations about participating in the plans for the economic and social reconstruction of Western Europe, a process which was closely associated with the name of General George Marshall, the foremost advocate of American financial aid for Europe and of American support for European initiatives. (The importance of Marshall Aid for the beginning of Irish economic programming has already been discussed.) In July 1947 Ireland was represented at the Conference on European Economic Co-operation which opened in Paris. In these post-war years, the country was beginning to learn the first faint lesson that her destiny might have to be worked out in a European context as well as in an Anglo-Irish one. She was the first country to agree to accept the jurisdiction of the Court of Human Rights: she was also a founder member of the Council of Europe which provided a forum for ideas of European unity that were later embodied in the Treaty of Rome. Unfortunately, Ireland also regarded the Council as an airing-place for her grievance about partition, but as the futility of a 'sore thumb' policy was realised, it was gradually dropped.

Domestically, the most controversial episode in the history of the first coalition was the 'mother-and-child scheme' crisis. Dr Noel Browne of Clann na Poblachta was given the Ministry of Health on his first day as a Dáil deputy. He brought to his duties a vigour and a zeal which led to extensive changes in public health, notably in the virtual eradication of tuberculosis as a killer disease. More generally, he wanted to develop the health services at large. Public health was one of those areas where there had been little progress under native government: the inadequacies of the dispensary and hospital services bore heavily on the poor. Fianna Fáil had brought in the Health Act of 1947 as the basis of a national health service. Browne now attempted to give effect to some of the provisions of that Act. Being particularly concerned about the high figures for infant mortality, he was anxious to provide maternity treatment, and medical attention for children up to the age of sixteen, free of charge and without the operation of a means test.

Not surprisingly, the scheme encountered opposition from the medical profession which had great prestige in Irish society and which was organised in a powerful pressure group of conservative interests, the Irish Medical Association. The IMA condemned the 'mother-and-child scheme', referring to the dangers of socialised medicine and political control, claiming the scheme would interfere with the doctor-patient relationship and objecting to the absence of a means test. However, it was not to be a straight fight between the Minister and the doctors, as in Britain: the opposition to the scheme received formidable support from the Roman Catholic hierarchy which had already, unknown to Browne and the coalition cabinet, voiced its disapproval to Mr de Valera of parts of the 1947 Act. In a letter of 10 October 1950 the bishops' objections to the mother-and-child scheme were conveyed to the Taoiseach, Mr Costello. The powers to be given to the state under the scheme would be, in their view, 'in direct opposition to the rights of the family and of the individual and are liable to very great abuse . . . If adopted in law they would constitute a ready-made instrument for future totalitarian aggression. The right to provide for the health of children belongs to parents, not the State. The State has the right to intervene only in a subsidiary capacity, to supplement, not to supplant'. The bishops were particularly opposed to the proposal that local medical officers should give sex education to Catholic girls and women, a proposal which might well lead to 'provision for birth limitation and abortion'.

In the period that followed, Browne believed that he had met the bishops' objections to the scheme. 'I should have thought it unnecessary', he wrote to the Taoiseach at one stage, 'to point out that from the beginning it has been my concern to see that the mother-and-child scheme contained nothing contrary to Catholic moral teaching.' With regard to sex education he promised he would 'provide any safeguards in matters of health education as would meet the requirements of the Hierarchy'. After much confusion and misunderstanding, it was clear by March 1951 that the bishops' suspicions were still unallayed. Costello informed Browne that the government could not stand behind a scheme which the bishops found objectionable in respect of Catholic teaching. Browne, however, stood firm, particularly in rejecting a means test, and was finally asked to resign by Seán MacBride, his colleague in government and leader of the Clann na Poblachta party. (The request, it is interesting to note, did not come from Mr Costello – an example of the strength of party leaders within the coalition, and the relative weakness of the Taoiseach.) Browne complied with the request on 12 April 1951, bitterly upbraiding MacBride as he did so and releasing the correspondence on the affair to the press so that the whole episode immediately became a matter for public debate. There followed an embittered discussion in the Dáil from which the Fianna Fáil opposition remained astutely aloof. Rank-and-file supporters of the Clann party were dismayed by the head-on clash of its two representatives in government and by the apparent alignment of the leader and other prominent members of an allegedly radical party with clericalist and conservative pressures. Defections from the Clann parliamentary group changed the balance in the Dáil and led to a dissolution in May 1951.

In a celebrated editorial on Browne's resignation, *The Irish Times* commented: 'This is a sad day for Ireland. It is not so important that the mother-and-child scheme has been withdrawn to be replaced by an alternative project embodying a means test. What matters more is that an honest, far-sighted and energetic man has been driven out of active politics. The most serious revelation however is that the Roman Catholic Church would seem to be the effective government of this country.' Coming from a newspaper which was still more Protestant and post-Unionist than liberal in flavour, such a comment might be regarded as jaundiced and exaggerated. Yet it raised a central question on which the other dailies maintained a pusillanimous editorial silence. The bishops' apologists then and thereafter made the point that the hierarchy made no attempt to publicly embarrass the government. Their critics retorted that backstairs diplomacy was worse than an open stand and also accused the hierarchy of promoting the vested interests of a conservative professional group. The truth is that the bishops, of whom Archbishop McQuaid of Dublin was the most formidable representative, *did* act out of a genuine concern for moral principles but it was the fussy concern of cautious men remote from harsh social realities, influenced by an unrealistic sociology and almost neurotically fearful of state encroachment and creeping Communism. Their views on health and social welfare had been running counter for over a decade to the centralising tendency of the Department of Health and the conflict had now come to a head. Put another way, the Catholic moral code had in practice been enshrined in the law of the state since the 1920s, and to the bishops the mother-and-child scheme seemed the first overt challenge to their moral domination.

Browne's fall and the abandonment of the scheme cannot be attributed exclusively to episcopal influence – no more than can, say, Parnell's destruction in 1891. The 1951 crisis was aggravated by other factors – the peculiar conditions of coalition government, Browne's deteriorating relationship with MacBride, the confused course of the negotiations and correspondence with the bishops, the pressures of the IMA and – a point insufficiently emphasised – the genuine doubts of Browne's own colleagues on the economic feasibility of the scheme. But at bottom it was a Church-State crisis, the first since independence. It was to be a pyrrhic victory for the bishops: some of them at least were soon aware that they had overreached themselves; and consultations with the next administration on a new Public Health Bill were handled much more circumspectly. The public debate in the wake of the crisis was surprisingly vocal and it was the first time widespread interest had been aroused on something other than sterile constitutional issues. Anti-clericalism, hitherto a minority vein in modern Irish Catholic tradition, was strengthened. The dissident few, including Browne, who maintained then and thereafter that the bishops were hopelessly wrong (and who were to be finally vindicated by the episcopal welcome for a government proposal for a free health scheme in 1973) became convinced that the Irish Church was an incorrigible agent of reaction. The more liberal successors of the 1951 bishops were to find it difficult to lay the embarrassing ghost of the mother-and-child scheme. Much more important, Northern Unionists believed the episode proved the Republic to be a theocratic state, a belief which remained unshaken long after the Catholic bishops had ceased to be the powerful influence they once were.

Between 1948 and 1951 Clann na Poblachta suffered a catastrophic decline. Unfortunately, though the party could claim much credit for the achievements of the 1948-51 administration, its performance in the coalition revealed its immaturity and lack of discipline as well as the rivalry and jealousy among its leading members. The mother-and-child controversy threw the party into final disarray. At the 1951 general election, the electorate gave its verdict: the party's share of the popular vote dropped from 13 per cent to 4 per cent and its Dáil strength fell from ten seats to two.

The election of May 1951, though made inevitable by the consequences of the mother-and-child scheme crisis, was not directly brought about by the clash of Church and State but by the defection of two deputies over the government's refusal to increase the price of milk. This mundane factor set the tone of the election that followed. In spite of the high drama of the recent controversy and the sensational declaration of the Republic, the campaign topics were bread-and-butter ones, an indication that economic issues would dominate in future. The results disclosed an interesting new voting pattern. Though Fianna Fáil, not surprisingly, gained 4.4 per cent on its 1948 first preference votes, it secured only one extra seat. The explanation was a new electoral phenomenon, the appearance of a coalition attitude among voters. Solid coalition voting was evident in the distribution of preferences and it was clear that the electorate recognised a new, albeit temporary, choice – Fianna Fáil versus the rest. Fine Gael profited most from the trend, gaining nine seats at the expense of the smaller parties.

When the Dáil reassembled, Mr de Valera was elected Taoiseach with the support of Browne and some Independent deputies. Ruling with a minority government for almost three years, he was understandably anxious to avoid controversial policies. Nevertheless after complex and discreet consultations with the bishops (both for political and personal reasons de Valera was always anxious to avoid confrontation) a Health Act was passed in 1953 which was the basis of the health services until a new Health Act in 1970. An Adoption Act was also passed in 1952, once it had become clear that the hierarchy would not oppose such a measure provided certain safeguards in respect of faith and morals were assured: thus significantly one section of the Act laid down that the adopting parents were to be 'of the same religion as the child and his parents or, if the child is illegitimate, his mother'. The area of social welfare was rather less controversial than that of health, and the Social Welfare Act of 1952 passed into law with relative ease. It was a milestone insofar as it unified and extended welfare benefits, rationalising under the relatively new Department of Social Welfare widows' and orphans' schemes, national health insurance and unemployment insurance. Henceforth, the state was sponsor and part-financer of a compulsory insurance system to which employers and employees made weekly contributions. The Act also increased social assistance benefits for the self-employed, such as small farmers, thus satisfying the views of Catholic social teaching as well as Fianna Fáil political strategy. But the low *level* of the benefits payable made it clear that Irish governments were both unwilling to entertain and unable to implement a welfare state policy. The Irish poor would still have to rely heavily on the charity of their better-off neighbours.

The Fianna Fáil minority government of the 1951-54 period was as unsuccessful as its coalition predecessor and successor in dealing with the chronically depressed economy. In the spring of 1954 by-election results indicated waning support for the government and when Mr de Valera called a general election there existed no issue which Fianna Fáil could turn to its advantage. The campaign was simply an exercise in competing promises to the electorate. Fianna Fáil lost 4 seats (from 69 in 1951) and now stood at its lowest strength since 1932. Fine Gael maintained its remarkable recovery, moving from 40 seats in 1951 to 50 in this election, while Labour went from 16 to 19 seats. Though the parties had fought the election independently, it came as no surprise when Mr Costello now formed his second coalition administration. Among his ministers were such new figures as Gerald Sweetman (Fine Gael) in Finance, Liam Cosgrave (Fine Gael – and son of W. T. Cosgrave) in External Affairs, and Brendan Corish (Labour) in Social Welfare. Though the second coalition was more compact and less fragmented than the first (on this occasion the three-man Clann na Poblachta party supported, but did not participate in the government) and though Costello's position as Taoiseach was perhaps stronger on this occasion, the administration was less talented and lacked the initiative and enthusiasm which had marked the first experiment in inter-party government.

Even though the 1950s were years of economic and psychological gloom, the first diffident step away from claustrophobic insularity was taken in 1955 when Ireland became a member of the United Nations. At home the overall economic picture remained dreary and the government's attempts to counter inflation and the trading imbalance by increased taxation, severe import levies and decreased expenditure were predictably unpopular as well as failing to come to fundamental grips with the country's economic malaise. The repercussions of the Suez crisis in 1956 aggravated the general situation and a renewal of IRA activities added to the government's problems.

After the disarray of the 1940s the IRA underwent a remarkable resurgence in the 1950s. Part of the explanation lay in the resentment among young nationalists at the Ireland Act (1949), the excitement generated by the anti-partition campaign and the moral drawn by extremists from the campaign's futility. There began to emerge new leaders, dedicated and efficient organisers of the second IRA generation. The participation of Clann na Poblachta in 'Free State' politics alienated republican sentiment while the presence of republicans in the government made firm handling of the IRA difficult. Minimal co-operation between Northern and Southern police from 1948 onwards favoured IRA activity. Perhaps the most important factor in IRA recruitment was that the organisation offered a perennial escapist outlet to young men seething with the frustrations of living in an isolated, truncated country with a stagnant economy. The common Southern view of partition as British occupation of 'our six counties' was, in part, the product of the 'history' classroom but it owed much more to a general and long-standing nationalist ignorance of the North, compounded by the political platform and the popular press.

Against this background, IRA leadership determined on a Northern campaign, while ruling out the use of force against 'Free State' soldiers and police. The disastrous campaign began in the last months of 1956 and on New Year's Day 1957 two young militarists, Seán South and Fergal O'Hanlon, were fatally wounded during a raid on Brookeborough Barracks in Co. Fermanagh. The campaign was soon to peter out but while it lasted it was a serious crisis for Costello. In January 1957 the Taoiseach promised that the full resources of the state would be used to prevent further raids. In the same month the diminutive Clann na Poblachta group withdrew its support from the coalition and MacBride condemned the government on general grounds and for its inaction on partition.

The second coalition perished in this sea of economic and political troubles and a general election took place in March 1957. For the first time since 1927, Sinn Féin – the political wing of the IRA – contested a 'Free State' election. The cross-border raids and the deaths of South and O'Hanlon secured for them a large, though transient, sympathy vote (66,000) and 4 Dáil seats which the party refused to take. However, Sinn Féin participation was only a minor theme of the 1957 election : the real issue was the grim economic position which caused the electorate to put once more its almost despairing trust in de Valera's party. There was a significant swing back to Fianna Fáil of 5 per cent and the party won 78 seats, a comfortable overall majority of 10. Fine Gael lost 10 seats and Labour 7 while Clann na Poblachta was virtually wiped out. MacBride was not returned, though his party was to maintain an almost nominal existence up to 1965, formally dissolving itself in that year.

7 The National Recovery from 1958

The 1957 election was to usher in a sixteen-year period of Fianna Fáil dominance. More immediately, de Valera's new government, strong in its Dáil majority, moved firmly against the IRA by invoking Part 2 of the Offences against the State Act which provided for arrest and detention without trial. In a period when public opinion was not very concerned with civil rights there was no popular outcry when scores of republicans were interned in the Curragh camp. Though the Northern campaign was to continue nominally until 1962 the threat of violence had been effectively dealt with in the South by the end of 1957.

Assured of its parliamentary strength and sharply conscious of the political instability of the previous ten years, the government in 1958 decided to attempt to change the electoral system which made clear-cut parliamentary majorities so difficult to obtain. The bill to amend the electoral system, proposing to replace P.R. by the 'straight' vote, predictably passed through the Dáil but early in 1959 was rejected in the Senate by one vote. It was the first time since its establishment under the 1937 Constitution that the Senate had taken such a step and it is arguable that the move helped to harden public opinion against the amendment proposal. A referendum was arranged, concurrently with a presidential election, for 17 June 1959. De Valera, now 77 years old and all but totally blind, was leaving the active political stage he had dominated so long, and Fianna Fáil, nominating him for the presidency, mounted an intense double campaign with the slogan 'Vote Yes and de Valera!' The strategy was transparent but de Valera also felt that the proposed constitutional change would have the best chance of acceptance if it were clearly seen that he had no intention of being head of government again. Though he won the presidential election by a comfortable (12 per cent) majority, the electorate made the sophisticated political distinction which Fianna Fáil had hoped to blur and the constitutional amendment was lost by 52 per cent to 48 per cent. Pro-P.R. interests had fought a vigorous campaign with trade union backing and their majority in Dublin and Cork was decisive. A second Fianna Fáil-sponsored attempt to abolish P.R. was to be resoundingly defeated in a referendum in 1968.

Mr de Valera was destined to serve two presidential terms (being re-elected in 1966) with great distinction and he carried out his duties in a scrupulously non-political fashion. It may well be that he made his own opinions discreetly known during the dramatic period of the Northern upheaval from 1969 onwards, but the contemporary historian feels confident in asserting that the de Valera age in Irish history decisively ended in 1959. Even not excepting O'Connell, no leader had held the political stage so long: he dominated Irish politics, in or out of power, from the Clare by-election of 1917 to the years of neutrality and beyond. From the time of the Treaty split, he fiercely polarised emotions in nationalist Ireland but in the end perhaps won the respect of those who did not love him. In many ways representative of, and responding to, the feelings of the plain people of Ireland, he nevertheless turned to good electoral advantage an aura of enigma, austerity and even slight exoticism. Shrewd parliamentarian, able political strategist, constitutionally imaginative to the point of genius, his political touch was at times assured and brilliant (his leadership of the reconstituted Sinn Féin, his handling of the Blueshirts, his direction of neutrality), at other times uncertain to the point of disaster (his American tour, his absence from the Treaty negotiations, his behaviour from the Treaty split to the Civil War). In Dublin all his adult life, his vision was of, and his strength lay in, rural Ireland. Admirably statesmanlike and courageous at international level, as was evident in his League of Nations stances and his determination not to be stampeded by a pro-Franco hysteria during the Spanish Civil War, he was either unable or unwilling to change the climate of cultural insularity and intellectual repressiveness at home. Though concerned to demonstrate the state's impartiality towards different denominations, his own fervent Catholicism did not dispose him to challenge clerical and clericalist control in areas such as censorship, education and health. Strongly moulded by Gaelic League influences in his youth and absolutely committed to the ideal of restoring the Irish language, he never succeeded in infecting even his admirers with his enthusiasm, perhaps because it took the form of a rather bookish Gaelic League devotion and was divorced from the harsh realities of social and economic life in the Gaeltacht areas. His dream of a frugal, good-living and Gaelic new Jerusalem, enunciated *par excellence* in his 1943 St Patrick's Day speech, remained peculiarly his own. He had no burning passion to redress social inequities. But his greatest tragedy was his failure to comprehend the North. For him the Six-County area was essentially the fourth green field, and the task of unification was the recovery of the lost national territory. He believed the development of a sovereign Twenty-Six counties would lead ultimately to the unity he passionately desired; in fact the creation of a virtually homogeneous Catholic state of which he was prime architect, proved to be the greatest hindrance to that unity. In the end he would be remembered as a great leader of the Irish Catholic people, though failing fully to articulate even *their* aspirations.

The late 1950s and the early 1960s witnessed a decisive turning point in the history of the Irish polity. The forces of change were already at work when de Valera was succeeded as Fianna Fáil leader and as Taoiseach by Seán Lemass, but the succession eloquently symbolised the process of change, for Lemass epitomised the new Ireland as well as being in large measure its architect. As far back as the 1930s he had been an efficient Minister for Industry and Commerce and had been equally successful in ensuring essential supplies during the war years. Now almost sixty, his accession to leadership had been long delayed but for seven years he was to direct energetically the transformation of the economy, if not of society as a whole. His bent was pragmatic and his temperament instinctively managerial. For him economic progress was *the* priority: civil war memories and constitutional niceties mattered as little as did his predecessor's idyll of a rural, Gaelic society. He continued as Taoiseach after the general elections of 1961 and 1965 (the Fianna Fáil minority government of 1961 was arguably the best administration in the history of the state) and gave every encouragement to the new men in his party's leadership that were at last edging out the old guard. With young lieutenants like Jack Lynch, Charles Haughey, Donough O'Malley and George Colley, Fianna Fáil took on the smooth, slick and successful image of the 1960s.

The remarkable economic expansion of the Lemass era has to be set against the stark background of the middle 1950s. This was a period of unprecedented gloom and depression. No longer could the state of the economy be attributed to colonial misgovernment or wartime restrictions. Economic growth was non-existent, inflation was apparently insoluble, unemployment rife, living standards low, and emigration approaching 50,000 a year, a figure not far below the birth rate. Even some who were securely employed threw up their jobs to seek a new life in countries which held out brighter prospects for the future of their families.

The dawn that slowly broke over this dismal night was heralded not by some dramatically sudden development nor by some charismatic public figure but by an expert working in the relative obscurity of the civil service. T. K. Whitaker was appointed in 1956 to the key post of Secretary of the Department of Finance by the second coalition government but his role became significant only after Fianna Fáil resumed office in 1957. In his own words, 'the growing comment on the absence of a comprehensive and integrated programme is tending to deepen the all-prevalent mood of despondency about the country's future'. His ideas for such a programme were outlined in 'Economic Development' which was rapidly written, and published in May 1958 as a government White Paper. His proposal for a planned development of the Irish economy won the interest and approval of de Valera, then Taoiseach, and of Dr James Ryan, one of the Fianna Fáil old guard and a shrewd minister for finance. The White Paper was the basis for the First Programme for Economic Expansion, adopted in November 1958. It is significant that it was Lemass who was Taoiseach when it was implemented. Heretofore the state's approach to economic policy had been conservative in the extreme. Budgets had to be balanced, corrective measures taken against adverse swings in the balance of payments, and thrift and caution highly prized. The commercial banks which strongly influenced policy held most of Ireland's external assets, in the form of short-term sterling investment. Now there was to be a complete change. The programme noted that 'in our present circumstances we must be prepared to take risks under all headings – social, commercial and financial – if we are to succeed in the drive for expansion'. The commercial banks were pressured by the government into supporting economic expansion as the main national objective, while the powers and role of the Central Bank were to be enlarged. The development programme stated priorities in investment and there was particular concentration on the nurturing of export industries, and to this end generous tax incentives were held out to attract foreign capital and expertise. New public bodies specifically concerned with development were established. The programme also envisaged agricultural expansion though the results in this vital sector were to remain disappointing for several more years.

Never before had the state committed itself to a comprehensive and rational plan for the economy as a whole. It was a new departure also in the more fundamental sense of moving radically away from the old Sinn Féin philosophy of self-sufficiency and industrial protection, which, the programme warned, 'can no longer be relied upon as an automatic weapon of defence'.

The programme in itself could hardly have *created* prosperity in the early 1960s had not external trading conditions been buoyant, but at the very least it provided the *framework* of an impressive expansion of the economy in the five-year period from November 1958. From a position of no growth at all, national output increased between 1958 and 1963 by nearly one quarter and the purchasing power of wages rose by one-fifth. Unemployment fell by one-third and, most heartening of all, emigration in the 1961–66 inter-censal period was reduced to about 40 per cent of its level in the 1956–61 period. Twice as many factories were established between 1958 and 1963 as in the previous five-year period. While investment was doubled there was also a substantial increase in savings, a significant index of increasing public confidence. Economic success was paralleled by a strengthening of the national morale. The 1966 census showed a population increase of 62,000. Even more significant were the important changes in the various age groups disclosed by that census. The 20-24 age group had grown by nearly 25 per cent and there were also increases in the younger age groups. It was clear that considerably more people were staying at home and this, of course, increased the marriage rate as well.

As the First Economic Programme was nearing completion, the Second Programme, intended to cover the period up to 1970, was already being planned. There were reports from new planning bodies on Irish industry and manpower. 'Adaptation Councils' were set up to modernise particular industries and a Manpower Authority was established to deal with the question of labour resources, retraining and resettlement. The Second Programme set targets in the farming industry as well, while greatly increasing state aid to agriculture. In the event the Second Programme was far from being the success of its predecessor. Ireland's vulnerable dependence on British trade was demonstrated in October 1964 when Britain, as a corrective to her own economic crisis, imposed a 15 per cent levy on imports. The old ailment of an adverse balance of payments manifested itself again in 1965. Government financing of economic development involved a heavy increase in taxation. A serious situation of inflation was aggravated by an over-generous wages agreement in 1965, and temporary refusal of the country's admission to the Common Market after application had been decided upon, was another setback.

Moreover, though the standard of living rose for all, progress towards social justice was disappointing and there still remained grave discrimination in areas such as housing, education and health. Yet, whatever the blemishes of the new Irish society, it was clear that a corner had been dramatically and irreversibly turned in the early and mid-1960s. The turning point was by no means restricted to the economy. Factories, new housing schemes and more consumer goods were impressive enough evidence of progress but not nearly as important in their social significance as the remarkable increase in the number of motor-cars and the introduction of television. The motor-car did much to break down the suffocating insularity and monotony of Irish rural and small-town life. Inevitably there would in time be a debit side to this process as local loyalties and the sense of 'parish' identity would weaken: for the moment, geographical mobility contributed greatly to the increasing popularity of Gaelic games and of traditional Irish music.

After a long period of conservatism, repressiveness and censorship, there began in the 1960s a new frankness of discussion, a spirit of positive self-criticism, a liberalisation of religious thinking with the pontificate of John XXIII, an increase in intellectual maturity, and a rejection of paternalism. It is arguable that the single most powerful agent of change in the moulding of new attitudes was the introduction of a national television service. A national radio service had been a deservedly popular institution since the 1920s – it had striven with great success to reflect what was distinctive on Irish life and culture – but the government was reluctantly compelled to make a decision in 1960 to set up Telefís Éireann (Irish Television) to defend a crumbling Irish cultural distinctiveness against the growing popularity of British television in Dublin and along the east coast. The reluctance sprang partly from doubts about the economic feasibility of the project but also perhaps from a presentiment that such a service would have incalculable political and cultural consequences on Irish life and attitudes. The Broadcasting Act set up an Authority to administer the service, which was to be self-supporting, deriving its revenue from commercial advertising as well as from licence fees. The government and in particular the Minister for Posts and Telegraphs adopted an attitude of prudent supervision over the service. This was illustrated, for example, by Lemass's forthright statement that television was an instrument of public policy and by provisions in the Act for direct access to television facilities by government ministers whenever it was deemed desirable, and for official censorship of the views of subversive and illegal organisations.

The service made an enormous and almost immediate impact on Irish life. While bringing to Irish homes the vulgar triviality of 'canned' Anglo-American programmes, it also relieved the drabness of much of Irish life and shattered the cosy complacency of traditional Irish attitudes. Subjects which had been virtually taboo – the place of the Church in Irish society, for example – were widely aired in popular programmes, and received with pleasurable shock by the viewing public. It is difficult to conceive of a more radical force in the maturing of Irish society.

It is not without significance that one of the first major public events to be covered by the national television service was the visit to Ireland of the American President, John F. Kennedy, in the summer of 1963, a few months before his tragic assassination. The ease and charm of the young President, and his obvious happiness at being in Ireland, evoked the acclaim of a people not latterly given to demonstrations of political enthusiasm. The highlight of his visit was his address to both houses of the Oireachtas,

146

which was notable for his expression of approval of the role which Ireland had been playing in international affairs. But the Kennedy visit had a deeper significance. The President was the descendant of Irish Catholic emigrants: his success symbolised the endurance and tenacity of the post-Famine Irish. It was peculiarly appropriate that he should have visited Ireland at a time of resurgence and a new national self-esteem.

Perhaps the most exciting departure in the state's search for maturity was the development of an independent foreign policy in the years after 1957. In a sense the country had been striving for independence in foreign affairs ever since 1922 but the success of the wartime neutrality policy indicated what the role of Ireland might be in the period when the Cold War dominated international politics and the sensitive, emergent Afro-Asian states were determined to have no part in the war of nerves and propaganda between East and West. When Ireland was admitted to the United Nations in 1955, it seemed at first as if 'the free world' had automatically gained one more cipher in the voting lobbies at the UN. Thus, Cosgrave, External Affairs Minister at the time, though indicating in the Dáil Ireland's intention to 'avoid becoming associated with particular blocs or groups so far as possible', was emphatic that 'we belong to the great community of states made up of the U.S., Canada and Western Europe'. With Fianna Fáil's return to power, however, Mr Frank Aiken was given the External Affairs portfolio which he was to hold until 1969. He patronised, if he did not initiate, a new departure which was implemented by the bright young men who had joined the foreign service in the late 1940s. Briefly, the spirit of the new policy was constructive and involved non-alignment: it was felt that Ireland, uniquely placed as a Western nation with no murky imperial past and with a strong anti-communist attitude, might well play a significant, independent role at the United Nations.

Thus Aiken and the Irish delegation argued volubly for a treaty to limit the spread of nuclear weapons – a cause also dear to the Afro-Asians – and pleaded for a discussion in the Assembly on the question of the admission of 'Red' China (The People's Republic of China) to the United Nations, while condemning Chinese aggression in Tibet. The independent Irish attitude evoked indignation in conservative Irish-American circles. A more effective and impressive aspect of Ireland's independent policy, however, was her contribution to the peace-keeping operations of the United Nations. Her universal acceptability in this role was sufficient vindication of her foreign policy and, from the late 1950s onwards, Irish soldiers gave service to world peace in the Middle East, the Congo, Cyprus and Kashmir.

But an independent foreign policy, after all, was a luxury for a small and poor nation, increasingly vulnerable in a world of ever-more interdependent trading blocs and communities. So it was that an anxiety not to offend the more powerful nations of the West had already become evident by 1961, as Ireland turned her eyes towards the European fleshpots. That an adventurous and exciting foreign policy was going to be considerably modified became very clear in 1961 when Ireland voted against the admission of 'Red' China to the UN, and again in 1962 when Lemass warmly praised the United States as the guardian of the 'free world' and unequivocally condemned the 'communist bloc'.

Independence in foreign affairs was, therefore, to a certain extent an illusion. So was the old Sinn Féin dream of economic independence. The Republic moved inexorably away from the shelter of her tariff walls into wider trade structures. The country participated in the 'Kennedy Rounds' of general tariff reductions and then in December 1965 came the free trade agreement with Britain. Britain was to abolish virtually all restrictions on Irish imports by July 1966 and would greatly increase the Irish share of the British market for agricultural products. For her part, the Republic undertook to dismantle gradually tariff barriers against British goods and end the tax incentives and subsidies for foreign industrialists over a period of fifteen years.

148

These agreements were but the prelude to Ireland's entry into the Common Market. In 1971–72, the great debate took place on the advantages and disadvantages of joining the European Economic Community. As the time drew near for a national referendum on entry, an intense campaign was mounted by pro- and anti-Marketeers. In its appeal to the electorate to approve of entry, the Fianna Fáil government was supported by Fine Gael, the main opposition party (one of whose leading members, Dr Garret FitzGerald, was the most persuasive and eloquent advocate of entry) and uneasily opposed by a far from united Labour Party. The largest single occupational group in support of entry was the farming community which was dazzled by the glittering prospect of an undreamt-of prosperity in a Community prepared to pay high prices for Irish meat. Against entry were the negligible and fragmented forces of the left. Advocates of membership emphasised the need to escape from economic isolation, the futility of remaining outside such a dynamic trading bloc, the prosperity which the farming community would experience, the diversified markets to be found by Irish quality exports, the benefits that would accrue to the country from the Community's regional and social policies, and, less convincingly, Ireland's 'destiny' as a European country. The Northern dimension was also given some attention: the pro-Marketeers argued that British and Irish membership together would eventually facilitate Irish unification. But perhaps the most telling point of all was the crude, mundane and unpalatable fact that the country's heavy dependence on the British market made entry an almost inevitable consequence of the United Kingdom's membership. If Britain went in, and Ireland stayed out, the tariff barriers of the Community would be raised against her, and a total and agonising reappraisal of the economy would be called for.

The anti-Marketeers asserted that Ireland should face up to such a reappraisal. Appealing to the old, independent nationalist tradition, they argued that a decision not to join would end the slavish economic and cultural dependence on Britain and compel Ireland to seek out and develop contacts with non-European countries with whom Ireland had fundamentally more in common than with the materialist Babylon which, the anti-Marketeers insisted, was the real essence of the Community. Needless to say, what finally determined the issue was the failure of the anti-Marketeers to demonstrate convincingly that there was 'an alternative'.

In the event, the popular verdict, delivered on 10 May 1972, had the dimensions of a landslide, with 83 per cent of the voters declaring in favour of membership. Whatever consequences the momentous decision might have, it could at least be said that it was a resounding and emphatic one. Membership became effective on 1 January 1973. Twelve months afterwards, an interim and tentative profit-and-loss assessment of membership would have to include disappointment with the lack of progress in the Community's regional policy, grave concern at the effect of membership on raging inflation, cautious satisfaction that the predictions of widespread unemployment had proved unfounded and guarded optimism that dependence on the British market was beginning to be loosened.

As has already been made clear, Seán Lemass in his seven years as Taoiseach left his permanent mark on the new Ireland. His business was promoting economic prosperity rather than the redistribution of national wealth. Pro-American and pro-EEC, he tolerated rather than approved of Aiken's internationalism. Yet he was the man for the times and his practical statesmanship was best shown by his exchange of visits with Captain O'Neill, the Northern Ireland premier, in 1965. One of his final duties was to preside over the fiftieth anniversary celebrations of the 1916 Rising. Though the commemoration sparked off a new interest in James Connolly among the growing number of people concerned with social injustice in Ireland, it was on the whole an incongruous event in the Lemass age. 1916 seemed centuries away in 1966 and Mr de Valera's appeal for rededication to the 'national aims' of language revival and national unity seemed to embarrass the brisk young politicians of the new generation.

Lemass's impending retirement in 1966 was the signal for an intense power struggle for leadership of the Fianna Fáil party and for the office of Taoiseach. The prize went to Jack Lynch, a quiet-spoken and pleasant-mannered Corkman. A hurler of brilliance in the 1940s, Lynch had given up the bar for politics in 1948 and unobtrusively moved up the *cursus honorum* of cabinet posts to the Finance Ministry, meanwhile extending the popularity he had always enjoyed in his native city. Perhaps the secret of his success was the impression he gave of having power thrust upon him rather than seeking it out. In the 1969 general election he won back an overall majority for Fianna Fáil, despite the predictions of the pundits. The Labour programme for a socialist Ireland was rejected overwhelmingly by a cautious electorate, and Fianna Fáil's triumph was very much a personal victory for Jack Lynch whose whistle-stop convent circuit tour revealed him as a consummate campaigner. Though the result enormously strengthened his hand against his rivals, he was almost immediately beset by the repercussions of the Northern crisis.

During the next three or four tumultuous years, the absence of any positive Dublin policy on the North became painfully evident. Lynch's dismissal of two cabinet ministers on suspicion of arms-running, the resignation of another minister and the setting up of a splinter party, Aontacht Éireann, the sensational arms trial of the ex-ministers, the James Bond like atmosphere of espionage and intrigue, the convulsion caused in the South by Bloody Sunday, January 1972 in Derry, the burning of the British Embassy in Dublin – all these earth-shaking events still left Jack Lynch and Fianna Fáil solidly in office. Lynch had to face crisis after crisis in these years, and he reiterated Fianna Fáil's determination to seek reunification by peaceful means, constantly dissociating his party from the men of violence. He sponsored the removal of the controversial section on the Catholic Church's 'special position' from the Constitution, an amendment overwhelmingly approved by the voters in December 1972. Yet all this did not add up to anything like a Northern policy and Lynch failed to give any convincing notice of intent to make the long-delayed and essential changes in the law and attitudes of the South.

When Lynch called a general election for March 1973, his calculated gamble failed to come off. A favourite election theme of Fianna Fáil's was the success it claimed in keeping the Northern troubles from spilling over into the South. This seemed to many to be a cynical exploitation of the Northern convulsion. But what concerned the southern electorate was not so much the trauma of the North as inflation and rising prices and the universal feeling that it was time for a change after sixteen years of rule by a party which showed many of the signs of an irritating complacency, if not of arrogance. And now there *was* an alternative: Labour and Fine Gael overcame their dislike of coalition to offer the people an agreed 14-point programme, and the 'National Coalition' came to power by a narrow margin. Liam Cosgrave became Taoiseach, and Labour leader Brendan Corish was made Tánaiste, with government ministries being distributed in proportion to party strength. If not quite a ministry of all the talents, the new two-party government was certainly high-powered. It immediately made an impression by initiating a spate of ameliorative legislation and by seeming to move actively towards a peaceful solution of the Northern crisis, though after a year in office it was still dragging its feet on the controversial contraception issue and had yet to prove that it would crack down on the unpleasant activities of property speculators.

It seems safe to say that, well before the early 1970s, the former agonisings on whether independence was worth while had been stilled. Disenchantment there had been in plenty since the Civil War when the Sinn Féin vision of a brave new Ireland had receded. Even in the most favourable circumstances the prospect for a revival of the Irish language had always been unpromising. The Gaeltacht areas steadily dwindled through neglect and emigration (as did the West as a whole). Not for decades was the central strategy of revival revealed as utterly mistaken – the assumption that the schools could successfully spread the language to society at large. Yet where there was much loss and waste there was certainly some profit. Without a state language policy, however defective, poets like Seán Ó Ríordáin, musicians like Seán Ó Riada, novelists like Máirtín Ó Cadhain might have forever remained silent. And, as the seventies dawned, a score of budding poets chose the ancestral tongue as their medium. All the evidence was that if the Irish language was really in a terminal illness, it would be an unconscionable long time dying.

Between the two literatures, Gaelic and Anglo-Irish, there lingered misunderstanding and suspicion. In a sense, Irish twentieth-century literature in English had been born of disillusion with the Gaelic vision. The whole world of 'Gaelic Leaguery' was brilliantly caricatured – in Irish – in Myles na Gopaleen's (*alias* Flann O'Brien) *An Béal Bocht*. It is true that Frank O'Connor bridged the two worlds in his splendid translations from the Irish and that Seán Ó Faoláin brilliantly evoked the lost Gaelic world in his biographies of Hugh O'Neill and Daniel O'Connell. Nevertheless the dominant note of the best Irish writing in English was a sardonic realism, a reflection of intellectual disenchantment with the narrowness of Irish life since independence. However, the early 1970s witnessed something of a *rapprochement* between writers active in Irish on the one hand and poets such as Thomas Kinsella and John Montague on the other.

In the early 1970s, the elderly Irishman in the street – or pub – might well ponder over the changes that had taken place in his lifetime. The Sinn Féin resurgence of his youth had given way to civil war, bitterness and disenchantment. Emigration, rural depopulation, unemployment and social injustice had been the ugly and chronic features of the state in which he had moved into middle age. The gradual achievement of political separation from Britain had not been matched by cultural and economic independence. If the insularity and provincialism of the earlier decades had now given way to more liberal attitudes, he might well regret the loss of the cosy pieties of an age when paternalism in Church and State protected his family from undesirable alien influences! His womenfolk were moving away from the nursery and the kitchen sink and beginning to demand equality. Churches were, for the most part, still thronged on Sundays but there was disturbing evidence that the intensity of religious belief and practice was diminishing. Sin and saintliness were no longer the certain categories they once had been.

Yet the poverty and drabness of the 1930s had gone. Improvements in living standards had benefited all, though some less than others. The Irish countryside had been modernised in many respects, not least by rural electrification. In the 1960s, with free post-primary education and a university student grant scheme, a belated beginning had been made towards equality of educational opportunity. A satisfactory national health scheme was also on the way. The haemorrhage of emigration had been staunched. The discovery of such rich mineral resources as lead and zinc and the more long-term prospect of oil and gas drillings in the Celtic Sea promised a new prosperity – provided the benefit accrued to the people as a whole. But in this otherwise reasonably bright sky the cloud of the Northern crisis continued to loom ominously.

8 Northern Ireland

From the 1920s to the late 1960s, at least, there are two histories of Ireland. North and South had very different developments, and for decades cross-border contacts were confined to limited areas, not the least being smuggling. The setting-up of a regional government and parliament for Northern Ireland within the United Kingdom derived, as we have seen, from the Government of Ireland Act 1920. The arrangement was accepted at the time by Ulster Unionists with a show of reluctance, but it was not long before they became attached to the settlement, seeing in it their strongest guarantee. Section Two of the Act provided for a Council of Ireland which would foster co-operation between Belfast and Dublin, but the Council was never set up and the partition which was intended to be temporary soon took on a very permanent air. The opening of the Northern Ireland Parliament in June 1921 made partition an accomplished fact months before the Anglo-Irish Treaty negotiations. In the course of these negotiations all attempts to involve the Ulster Unionists in Irish unity discussions met with failure. Sir James Craig stood firm on the constitutional position, encouraged no doubt by de Valera's statement in August 1921 that Sinn Féin would not use force to settle the Ulster question, and by the certain knowledge that coercion would never be applied by Britain. The signing of the Anglo-Irish Treaty was followed by heightened tension in the North, expressed in bloody riots. On the border there were clashes between the British military and the IRA. Both pro- and anti-Treaty groups participated in these incidents and Collins supplied arms for use by northern units. Indeed, this was the kind of struggle that might well have intensified, had a united Sinn Féin front been maintained in the South.

If Southern Irishmen were bitterly disappointed over the Boundary Commission debacle, Northern Nationalists simply could not accept the concept of partition as a permanent agreement and went through a phase of traumatic shock. Believing the Northern state would not last, the nationalist minority (perhaps 34 per cent of the population) refused to have anything to do with it. The initial phase of abstention was arguably a mistake because this was the period which saw the foundation of education and local government structures. These important developments remained uninfluenced by minority participation and constructive criticism. Abstentionism also reinforced the apartheid mentality between Protestants and Catholics in every department of life. As early as 1923 the Catholic bishops were protesting about the political and educational measures of the Northern government. They also objected to the abolition of proportional representation in local government elections and to the practice of gerrymandering – the artificial manipulation of ward boundaries so as to ensure unionist over-representation and control in local government areas where there was a natural nationalist majority, as in Derry City and Tyrone County Council.

Meanwhile, the Northern state established its regular police force (the Royal Ulster Constabulary) as well as a special constabulary, the 'B Specials', being part-time police who might become full-time in an emergency. The Civil Authorities (Special Powers) Act of 1922 was made permanent in 1933. The imposition of curfew, the exclusion of certain persons from Northern Ireland, the banning of organisations and the arrest and detention of suspected persons were only some of the sweeping powers which the Act conferred on the Minister for Home Affairs. To the nationalist minority the armed (and virtually all-Protestant) police force and the drastic Special Powers were instruments of Unionist oppression; to the Protestant majority they appeared as necessary safeguards in a position of permanent emergency where one-third of the population

[handwritten margin note: no one believed it could last!]

would not accept the legitimacy of the state and where the Irish Free State proclaimed territorial unification as its chief national aim.

As soon as it became clear that there was to be no change in the constitutional position, Nationalist M.P.s began to take their seats in the Northern Parliament (from 1932 housed in an impressive building at Stormont, outside Belfast), Joseph Devlin launching the National League of the North pledged to constitutional opposition, though he and his followers remained largely a futile group. The government meanwhile moved to strengthen its position against dissidents by abolishing in 1929 proportional representation for parliamentary elections. In 1925, Independents, Labour and Farmers had gained seats at the expense of the government which accordingly considered its majority to be in danger. But, in spite of repeated anti-partition propaganda, it may be doubted whether the abolition of P.R. substantially affected nationalist minority representation, just as it is difficult to prove that gerrymandering was at all significant in parliamentary, as distinct from local, elections. Nationalist representation suffered from the wide dispersal of support in rural areas and also from the divided allegiances of anti-Unionists, some sticking by the old-style nationalists, others giving their support to republicans. The consequence was that anti-Unionists generally held only 10-12 of the 52 Stormont seats, and 2 of the 12 Westminster seats.

We may remind ourselves here that the Government of Ireland Act had set very drastic limits to the power of the Northern Ireland Parliament. The Act made it clear that the Westminster parliament would still continue to exercise supreme authority: more specifically, the Northern Parliament could not legislate in the following spheres – income tax, customs and excise tax, political and trade relations with foreign states, the armed forces, peace and war, the postal service and the Supreme Court. (But it was Westminster neglect, not interference, that was a long-term cause of the upheaval of the late 1960s.) The financial provisions of the Government of Ireland Act were complicated and ramshackle and were the source of continuing difficulty for finance ministers in the North. However, in 1938 it was established that Britain would meet Stormont budget deficits, and this was to remain Northern Ireland's guarantee against financial collapse.

The area was particularly vulnerable to the harsh winds of post-war depression. Linen and shipping faced a rapidly diminishing market from the mid-1920s onwards. Employment in the Belfast shipyards dropped from 20,000 in 1924 to 2,000 in 1933. Throughout the 1930s an annual average of 25 per cent of the insured population was out of work. Agriculture, accounting for about one-quarter of all occupied persons, remained depressed and backward despite government aids and incentives. Bad housing and a low state of public health (tuberculosis was responsible for 46 per cent of the death-rate in the 15-25 age group in 1938) were the dreary concomitants of chronic poverty and unemployment.

A cut in outdoor relief rates in 1932 brought some Protestant and Republican trade unionists into temporary alliance but this had no significance in a community deeply polarised around historic hatreds and prejudices. Socialist policies and organisations made little impact on the Northern scene. Apart from the fact that the small scale of society and industry did not favour the advance of socialist doctrines, the Protestant worker regarded his Protestant boss as the protector of his British and Protestant heritage, and the Catholic worker as his economic, political and religious foe. The Orange Order with its vast membership spanning all sections of society – landed gentry, small farmers, industrial bosses and shipyard workers – gave the economically underprivileged Protestant the illusion of belonging to a superior 'Protestant people'. Unionist power was apparently monolithic, large numbers of seats were uncontested in elections and both in parliament and government many Unionists seemed to have a virtual life tenure. At general elections the Unionists had predictable and overwhelming majorities particularly when a cry of danger could be raised as in 1938 when the issue of partition at the

Anglo-Irish talks helped to return 39 Unionists to a parliament of 52. Meanwhile Catholic resistance had subsided into sullen resentment, though the viciousness of sectarianism flared occasionally into bloodshed as in Belfast in 1935 when rioting accounted for eleven deaths as well as widespread arson and malicious damage. Leaders of both communities did little to improve the harsh sectarian climate. Lord Craigavon's notorious phrase 'a Protestant Parliament for a Protestant people' was matched by Cardinal MacRory's egregious utterance that the Protestant Churches did not form part of the true Church of Christ. Catholics and Protestants kept themselves rigorously segregated in education and it is difficult not to regard the division of children as being a major factor in perpetuating the enmities of adults.

World War II had a dramatic impact on Northern Ireland, strengthening its constitutional position immeasurably and benefiting the economy. Not only did Ulster men and women participate fully in the war effort as a whole, but Southern neutrality gave Northern Ireland an immense strategic importance. Belfast, Derry and other places sheltered the escort vessels which guarded British-bound convoys and patrolled the north-western approaches. Later Derry became an important U.S. naval base and Northern Ireland as a whole was a training ground for American forces before D-Day as well as providing various air bases. The severe German air raids on Belfast in April-May 1941 brought death and injury to hundreds, caused much damage to property and temporarily crippled the shipyards of Harland and Wolff. The whole effect of Northern Ireland's participation in the war was to strengthen the link with Britain, buttress Unionism and place the North on a still more divergent path from the neutral South.

The conscription issue was a cause of much controversy in the North. Though Craigavon in 1939 proposed the extension of the measure to Northern Ireland, the Catholic bishops in the North gave warning of nationalist opposition. In 1941 the conscription issue was again raised. Northern Unionist leaders were divided on the practical wisdom of imposing the measure, some government members believing that the burdens of Britain at war should be fully shouldered, others fearing that conscription would have the undesirable result of training young nationalists in the use of arms as well perhaps as proving unpopular with many Unionists. In the event, the British government took the prudent decision to drop the matter altogether. The proposal to create a Local Defence Force also raised difficulties, Craigavon expressing the view that because there was a 'fifth column' in the state, 'we require to go very carefully along the road of arming people in Northern Ireland'.

While Northern self-government was further circumscribed by wartime exigencies and while the North experienced the prevailing austerities, the economy boomed. The traditional shipbuilding and engineering industries were kept at full stretch in the production of ships, tanks and bombers. In shipbuilding alone employment soared from 7,300 in 1938 to 20,600 in 1945. The textile industry also geared itself to wartime demands, mass-producing such items as uniforms, parachutes and tents. The build-up of American troops entailed a big programme of constructing barracks, laying down airfields and fitting out supply depots. Unemployment, then, was dramatically reduced but was by no means solved: in June 1943, at the height of the wartime boom, the rate was still 5% as compared with ½% in Britain. Agricultural productivity increased strikingly during the war and intensive cultivation involved a large labour force as well as widespread mechanisation. In comparison, progress in the South was slow. In both industry and agriculture, wages soared and savings accumulated as well.

The war also caused a certain shake-up in government circles. Within the cabinet itself, at an early stage, there was protest at the leadership's handling of issues like conscription and recruiting. In November 1940, Craigavon died and was succeeded as prime minister by a Unionist of similar calibre, J. M. Andrews. He made no significant cabinet changes and the administration continued to be blamed for its handling of the war effort, the economic situation following the air raids and other matters. After the government lost by-elections to Independent Unionists and Labour, a backbench revolt in the Unionist party led to Andrews' replacement in early 1943 by Sir Basil Brooke (later Lord Brookeborough), who brought fresh blood into the cabinet.

Change – at least social and economic change – was inevitable after the war. The appalling state of public health had been indicated by the poor physical condition of Belfast evacuees arriving at country centres, and a Ministry of Health was set up in 1944. The coming of the welfare state was to bring about a great transformation.

As early as May 1945, it was established that Northern Ireland would share the new British standards of social services. It was a Labour government which was to guarantee additional constitutional security to Northern Ireland by the Ireland Act of 1949 and it was the same government which would finance the new social services in the North. The Northern Ireland Health Services Act of 1948 ended the old system of dispensaries and poor law infirmaries, set up a General Health Services Board and instituted the same kind of comprehensive medical care which British citizens were enjoying. The problem of tuberculosis was at last attacked effectively and an ambitious scheme of hospital construction begun.

Despite the archaic Unionism of northern politics, increasing state intervention was the concomitant of the welfare state. Rail and road transport was brought under the public control of the Ulster Transport Authority in 1948. The Housing Acts of 1945 and 1946 provided for subsidies in both the private and public sectors.

The advances in health and social welfare benefits were, by Southern standards, spectacular and for the next two decades were to provide the strongest of all the material arguments against Irish unity. The contrast was equally striking in every field. The Education Act of 1947 was based on the British model, with free post-primary education being introduced and the school-leaving age being raised to 15. Generous university grants put real equality of educational opportunity substantially within the grasp of the Northern schoolchild at a time when it was still a pipedream for his Southern counterpart. The extension of higher level education in the North was to have one unforeseen and momentous consequence. In time, there emerged in the Catholic community highly articulate and politically sophisticated leaders who were determined to end what they considered to be the second-class status of the minority. Thus the Education Act of 1947 sowed dragon's teeth.

Whatever limited measure of independence was given Northern Ireland by the Government of Ireland Act was now further restricted. Fiscal freedom of action was further curtailed and financial estimates such as the Budget had to be put before the Treasury yearly and given prior approval. The welfare state had its opponents among Unionists, some of whom objected to its egalitarian philosophy and to its concomitant of high taxation. Nevertheless, Unionist M.P.s at Westminster managed to combine Tory opposition there with acceptance of increased social benefits at home.

The arrival of the welfare state in Northern Ireland in no way modified sectarianism or Unionist political hegemony. In the field of health, for example, the large and highly efficient Mater Hospital received no money from the Hospitals' Authority for either capital or current expenditure because it refused to relinquish its Catholic control and transfer its property to the Authority. Education was much more vitiated by sectarianism. Since the beginning of the state the government had attempted to bring all primary schools into the state system. The voluntary schools – the great majority of them Catholic – had resisted this attempt and were penalised by the withholding of all grants for capital expenditure: however in 1930 they were given grants of 50 per cent. At the time of the Education Act in 1947, grants totalling 65 per cent of capital expenditure were given to voluntary schools, both primary and secondary. Unionist backbenchers continued to be suspicious and critical of any concession to Catholic-controlled schools.

More generally, as the area of state and local authority patronage increased with the extension of social legislation, Catholics felt that the best positions and contracts in housing, health, transport and education were secured by government supporters. Unionists controlled local government for a number of reasons: the local government franchise was confined to the better-off citizen and there was a system of plural voting by limited companies. The control of housing, added to the fixing of ward boundaries, enabled Unionists to strengthen their hold over areas with overall Nationalist majorities – most notoriously, Derry City.

In 1963 Captain Terence O'Neill succeeded to the premiership vacated by Lord Brookeborough. O'Neill, of landed gentry stock, set out to reduce sectarian bigotry and to end the cold war with the South, while continuing to proclaim the permanence of the Border. He wished to give Unionism a more acceptable face but moderation was anathema to intransigent Unionists, and his policies evoked a strong reaction from Mr William Craig, a member of the cabinet, and from the Rev Ian Paisley, the forceful leader of the fundamentalist Free Presbyterian Church, a stoker of anti-popery fires, a magnetic demagogue and soon to be a politician of considerable astuteness. To Craig and Paisley, the 'Protestant Constitution' was sacrosanct and O'Neill the kind of heretic who is as obnoxious to the true believer as is the infidel without the gates.

In 1968 the simmering resentment of the minority boiled over with the first dramatic demonstrations of the Civil Rights Association. Ostensibly undenominational, the CRA represented the frustrations and the hopes of the Catholic minority who were no longer willing to tolerate second-class citizenship and various forms of discrimination. Though republicans were involved in the movement from the first, anti-partitionism was not one of its characteristics. Strongly influenced by the non-violent civil rights movement in the United States, the CRA songs and slogans

('one man one vote') were part of a universal currency –
'We shall overcome' rather than 'A Nation Once Again'
expressing their aspirations.

In August 1968 a march to Dungannon was designed to
draw attention to the iniquities of the housing allocation
system. Two months afterwards, on 5 October 1968, came
a dramatic confrontation between civil rights marchers and
police in Derry City, and violent baton charges took place
in support of a ban on the march by William Craig, the
Home Affairs Minister. Television cameras brought the
bloody clashes into the homes of startled Irish and British
viewers. Repression hardened the resistance of the minority.
Leaders such as John Hume and Austin Currie quickly
articulated the aims of the now determined Catholic minority while in Queen's University, Belfast, there emerged
the radical student movement – partly reflecting a world-
wide trend – called the People's Democracy whose objectives were not simply civil equality but eventually an all-
Ireland Workers' Republic. The prominent names here
were Bernadette Devlin, Michael Farrell and Éamon
McCann.

A promise of general reforms by the government and
Capt. O'Neill's dismissal of Mr Craig failed to solve the
tension. When, in the first days in 1969, the People's
Democracy organised a march from Belfast to Derry, the
marchers were violently attacked by Protestant extremists
at Burntollet Bridge. Against a background of growing
violence, a general election was held on 24 February,
resulting in the election of such civil rights leaders as
Hume and Ivan Cooper (the old-style Nationalists were
seen to be increasingly irrelevant) and also of Unionists
hostile to O'Neill. 'One man one vote' (universal adult
suffrage in local elections) was belatedly conceded by the
government in May 1969 but by now, in classic historical
fashion, the 'troubles' took on a momentum of their own.
Unionist resistance to reform brought about Capt. O'Neill's
resignation. His successor, Major James Chichester-Clark,
proved no more successful in dealing with the mounting
crisis.

Various incidents during the summer months (the explosive 'marching' period of the Orangemen) culminated in fierce rioting in mid-August 1969. In Derry there took place a three-day battle between the Royal Ulster Constabulary and rioters from the Catholic Bogside area, who sealed off 'no-go' areas. The mid-August troubles spread to Belfast where several lives – mostly Catholic – were lost. British troops were rushed to the trouble centres and it is significant that they were acclaimed by Catholics as their champions against Protestant extremists and the RUC. Military intervention from Westminster was followed by the British Home Secretary's (Mr James Callaghan) announcement of a reform programmme. The London initiative, though tragically slow to develop, seemed to some to be the beginning of the end for the Stormont regime. In the South the Taoiseach, Mr Lynch, asserted that Dublin could not ignore the plight of the Northern minority, and hospital field units were dispatched to the Border areas. However, southern inaction disappointed both those who hoped for the development of a positive policy on the North and those who expected a dramatic military intervention.

Another important consequence of the mid-August events should be noted. Throughout the 1960s the IRA leadership had directed the movement away from its traditional military role into political activism, arguing (as some of their predecessors did in the 1930s) that republicans should identify themselves with such popular grievances as poor housing and private control of fisheries. The traditional purists were uneasy about various aspects of the new policy – for example, increasing support for the recognition of existing political and legal institutions, and a growing Marxist influence on republican thinking. The traditionalists attributed the failure to defend the nationalist areas of Belfast during the August riots to a misguided policy of 'politicisation' in the IRA, and a split took place during the IRA Army Convention of December 1969 between the 'Officials' (those committed to the policies developed during the 1960s) and the 'Provisionals' (dedicated primarily to the urgent military problems at hand). The civil wing of the movement similarly divided the following month. Both sections retained the mystical description of Sinn Féin and in time came to be distinguished by reference to the Dublin streets wherein they had their respective headquarters. Though the Officials (Gardiner Place Sinn Féin) were to retain pockets of support in Belfast and other areas, the Provisionals (Kevin Street Sinn Féin) were soon to receive much stronger backing from republicans in the North itself, Britain and the United States.

In the first months of 1970 there were violent riots in Ballymurphy, a Catholic area in south-west Belfast. The indiscriminate use of C.S. gas on various occasions by the British Army had already begun to diminish its short-lived popularity. In June, the accession to power in Britain of the Conservatives under Edward Heath was quickly followed by a sharp deterioration in the Northern situation. In the same month, the British Army's failure to defend beleaguered Catholics against Protestant extremists in East Belfast was made good by local IRA men. In early July, intense rioting broke out when the Army carried out a curfew and arms search in the Catholic Lower Falls Road area. This marked the final alienation of the Catholic population from the British Army which was now regarded as bolstering up the discredited Stormont regime. The ineptitude of the Conservative government, and particularly of Reginald Maudling, the Home Secretary at this period, greatly aggravated the general drift from bad to worse. Chichester-Clark saw the solution in terms of an ever firmer enforcement of 'law and order'. Meanwhile, in August 1970, the moderate anti-Unionist M.P.s formed themselves into the Social Democratic and Labour Party. Led by a shrewd republican-labour politician, Gerry Fitt, the SDLP included such prominent civil rights leaders as John Hume, Austin Currie and Ivan Cooper.

On 6 February 1971 the first of some hundreds of British soldiers to die was killed by the IRA in Belfast. In March, Chichester-Clark resigned as Stormont premier and Unionist leader, to be succeeded in both capacities by Brian

Faulkner, destined to be one of the most durable and resilient politicians in the Northern scene. Distrusted by the Catholics and regarded as a compromiser by the Protestant working-class, he was to draw his strength from the moderate Unionists. A once monolithic Unionism was now fragmenting under the impact of the troubles. In April there began a systematic Provisional IRA bombing campaign which, with the exception of occasional truces, became a permanent and tragic feature of the violence. Though the Provisionals angrily denied that the campaign was of a sectarian nature and directed against civilians, this was the tragic, if unintended, outcome. The widespread damage to property and the killing and maiming of civilians aggravated still further the bitterness between the polarised communities in the North, caused Protestant extremists to retaliate in kind and contributed to the ever-present possibility of an all-out civil war.

On 8 July 1971 two young Derry men were shot dead by British soldiers. Leading members of the SDLP threatened to withdraw from Stormont unless there was a full-scale public inquiry into the two deaths. It was a dramatic ultimatum which arose from the necessity of winning back the political initiative from the IRA. Since no inquiry was forthcoming, Fitt was forced to lead his members out of the Northern Parliament on 16 July. The secession was a blow to the credibility of the Stormont system whose continuation had always depended on Catholic consent, no matter how resentful and sullen.

As violence escalated in the summer months and the number of explosions mounted (the most spectacular at this period being the IRA destruction of the huge *Daily Mirror* plant outside Belfast) there was a growing Protestant demand for the introduction of internment. The measure was finally brought in on 9 August 1971 with dawn swoops all over the North. The immediate consequence was days of bitter rioting. Not only was internment clumsily carried out and a total failure from the military point of view, but it united the whole Catholic population, as nothing else had done previously, in a total rejection of Stormont. The minority regarded internment as virtually an act of war and retaliated by withholding rents, rates and local taxes in a massive civil disobedience campaign which also indicated the disillusion of Catholics with the tardy steps to implement any real reforms in Northern life. Internment was a further and major stage in the disintegration of the Stormont system.

Between August and Christmas 1971 there was little or no lull in the violence. Though the province was now saturated with British troops, yet soldiers, policemen and UDR men (the Ulster Defence Regiment was a part-time security force) continued to be killed, civilians died in bomb blasts and gun battles, armed robberies were almost daily incidents and the social and business life of Belfast and other northern towns seemed to be grinding to a halt. At the end of September tripartite talks in Chequers between Heath, Lynch and Faulkner seemed to serve little purpose. In October 1971 the SDLP set up its 'alternative assembly': as a move to establish a rival parliament it was pretentious and ineffective but it was, for all that, another blow to Stormont.

At the turn of the year, speculation grew about a new British 'initiative' which proved disastrously slow in materialising. Then, on Sunday 30 January 1972, British Army paratroopers shot dead thirteen unarmed civilians during a civil rights demonstration in Derry. 'Bloody Sunday' finally convinced British politicians that a radical new departure in the North was essential. The angrily mourning Catholic community felt that the Army action in Derry was an outrageous attempt to enforce the authority of a tottering Stormont. It was now clear that the days of that discredited parliamentary rump were numbered. As William Craig rallied extremist Protestant opinion in the umbrella organisation called Vanguard, the British cabinet was already moving towards direct rule. On 24 March 1972 Edward Heath announced the proroguing of Stormont and the imposition of direct rule from Westminster. Though the suspension of the Northern Ireland Parliament was announced as a temporary measure, this was widely regarded as a piece of face-saving and it was equally widely understood that, no matter what the future might hold, the half-century of Unionist ascendancy had ended for ever. The reasons for the fall of Stormont were varied, but there was no doubting the major role played by the Provisional IRA. It was, consequently, a major blunder on the IRA's part not to have suspended its campaign at this stage. There was, it is true, a temporary truce in June–July 1972 while IRA leaders held abortive peace talks with William Whitelaw, who held, with cabinet rank, the newly-created post of Secretary of State for Northern Ireland and, as such, wielded virtually supreme power. But the atrocities went on. A series of operations was carried out by the IRA in Belfast on Friday 21 July (Bloody Friday) and nine people died in explosions. Ten days afterwards reinforced British troops poured into the nationalist areas of Derry and Belfast (Operation Motorman) and brought the 'no-go' districts back into control.

The violence continued during the period of direct rule. Protestant extremist groups, such as the open Ulster Defence Association and the illegal Ulster Volunteer Force, ignored calls for moderation and their activities were condoned in practice by such political figures as Ian Paisley and William Craig. Sectarian assassinations, often carried out seemingly at random, were the most horrific aspect of the violence. Mr Whitelaw worked doggedly towards – literally – a *modus vivendi*, assuring the Protestants there would be no tampering with the constitutional status of the North against their will and encouraging the Catholics to participate in a new future for the province. By now, the proliferation of Protestant 'extremist' or 'loyalist' associations bore witness to deep-seated Unionist fears of abandonment by Britain and of absorption by the Republic. The fears of abandonment were not groundless: British politicians and people alike had long since begun to tire of the seemingly insoluble Northern troubles.

On 20 March 1973 the British Government issued its White Paper on Northern Ireland which was subsequently given legal force in the Northern Ireland Constitution Act.

This provided for a new Assembly which, initially at any rate, would have even fewer powers than the old parliament but which, it was hoped, would lead to the formation of a power-sharing Executive, an entirely new concept in Northern politics. The Assembly elections were duly held and, towards the end of 1973, there painfully emerged a new alignment in Northern politics. A group of Assemblymen, consisting of the SDLP, Brian Faulkner's moderate Unionists and the middle-class bridge-building Alliance party, agreed to form a power-sharing Executive. Though the Executive, which was installed in office in the first days of 1974, could count on a precarious majority in the Assembly, the downright rejection of the power-sharing concept by anti-Faulkner loyalist members reduced the Assembly proceedings to a farce. Meanwhile, the Coalition government in Dublin, as well as the Fianna Fáil opposition, gave its moral support to the new developments. The Northern Ireland Constitution Act had also provided for the revival of the idea of a Council of Ireland, and a conference at Sunningdale in December 1973 (between Dublin, Belfast and London politicians) took the first tentative steps towards its establishment.

Within a few months however these fragile structures were dramatically destroyed. In the general election of February 1974, eleven of the North's twelve Westminster seats were captured by 'extreme' Unionists, and by May the newly-formed Ulster Workers' Council had launched a massive and successful loyalist strike against power-sharing and the Sunningdale agreement. With the Northern Ireland economy paralysed, the Executive collapsed. The new Labour Government in Britain temporarily resumed direct rule and embarked upon yet another 'initiative'. Elections would be held in the North, though not immediately, to choose the members of a constitutional convention where the conflicting groups would be encouraged to hammer out their own solution. Most observers feared that the conference would be a futile exercise.

By the autumn of 1974, about eleven hundred people had died in the Northern troubles since August 1969. Civilians had borne the brunt of the endless tragedy in lives lost and maimed, property destroyed and feelings brutalised. And still the Ulster question seemed more intractable than it had been in 1912. Yet a faint hope lay in the newly expressed strength of working-class loyalists, in their growing rejection of traditional Unionist leadership and in the beginnings of their awareness that poverty and ignorance had always been, in the end, the ultimate enemies which ordinary Protestants and Catholics shared across the religious divide.

To the contemporary observer in 1974, the Northern troubles had amazingly little impact on the South. There were, of course, such dramatic events as the resignation and dismissals of some of Mr Lynch's ministers in May 1970, followed by a sensational arms trial. There were gun-runnings and rumours of gun-running. There was the introduction of special criminal courts for the trial of IRA suspects, there were occasional tragic bombing incidents and there was some argument about Northern policy. But, by and large, there was no *popular* involvement, if we except the emotional outburst and the burning of the British Embassy in Dublin after Bloody Sunday in Derry. And there was no real indication (apart from the token gesture of deleting the 'special position' of the Catholic Church in Article 44) that the South wanted to change its constitution or its society to prepare itself for a new Ireland. Had a homogeneous Twenty-Six county sovereign state developed to the point where it no longer wished to consider the radically disturbing implications of a union of Catholic, Protestant and Dissenter?

Bibliographical Note

The last decade or so has seen the fruitful investigation of various aspects of Irish history since 1918. This select bibliography is, for reasons of space, largely confined to certain book-length studies but the reader should note that much valuable work on Irish society and political culture is to be found in such publications as *Studies*; *Administration*; *Political Studies*; and the *Economic and Social Review*. The twentieth-century section in T. W. Moody (ed.) *Irish Historiography, 1936–70* (Dublin 1971) should be consulted but this already requires to be brought up to date. Basic documents for our period include the Government of Ireland Act (1920), the Anglo-Irish Treaty of 1921, the constitutions of 1922 and 1937 and the official Dáil debates and minutes of proceedings.

The place of publication of all books mentioned below is London, unless otherwise stated.

Among the general works it would be perverse not to give pride of place to F. S. L. Lyons's magnificent *Ireland since the Famine* (1971), the second half of which deals with the 1918–69 period in considerable detail. Rather more than a third of O. MacDonagh, *Ireland* (Englewood Cliffs 1968) briefly surveys the new Ireland up to the 1960s and his sophisticated analysis will enrich the understanding of those already acquainted with the historical outline. T. P. Coogan, *Ireland since the Rising* (1966) is a journalist's pioneer work, readable and spirited. De Valera's career is, in a sense, the history of the time: the Earl of Longford and T. P. O'Neill, *Eamon de Valera* (1970) is the 'official' life and, though partisan and somewhat credulous, it incorporates material unavailable to previous biographers and faithfully reflects the thinking of the most important Irishman of our period. The Irish version, T. Ó Néill and P. Ó Fiannachta, *De Valera* (2 vols, Dublin 1968 and 1970), is fuller in many respects.

The concluding sections of a large number of works deal briefly with the 1918–23 period. These include J. C. Beckett's *The Making of Modern Ireland, 1603–1923* (1966); L. J. McCaffrey, *The Irish Question, 1800–1922* (Lexington 1968);

T. W. Moody and F. X. Martin (eds.), *The Course of Irish History* (Cork 1967); P. S. O'Hegarty, *Ireland under the Union, 1801–1922* (1952), only somewhat less forceful and impassioned than the same author's early polemic, *The Victory of Sinn Féin* (Dublin 1924); E. Strauss's Marxist interpretation, *Irish Nationalism and British Democracy* (1951); N. Mansergh's dispassionate *The Irish Question* (1965); and R. Kee, *The Green Flag* (1972) with its interesting examination of public attitudes to the growth of violence in 1920–21.

D. Macardle, *The Irish Republic* (1937: paperback 1968) has hardly been superseded as the 'republican' handbook of the revolutionary struggle and its useful appendices include Treaty documents. Also partisan is W. A. Phillips's 'unionist' approach in *The Revolution in Ireland, 1906–23* (2nd ed. 1926). E. Holt, *Protest in Arms: The Irish Troubles, 1916–23* (1960) is a good survey. T. D. Williams (ed.) *The Irish Struggle, 1916–26* (1966) is an important collection of essays. S. Ó Lúing, *Art Ó Gríofa* (Dublin 1953) is the most comprehensive life of Griffith though R. Davis, *Arthur Griffith and Non-Violent Sinn Féin* (Tralee 1974) has just appeared at the time of going to press. R. Taylor, *Michael Collins* (paperback 1961) is perhaps the most useful of several Collins biographies. R. B. McDowell has the definitive work on *The Irish Convention, 1917–18* (1970). B. Farrell, *The Founding of Dáil Éireann* (Dublin 1971) is original and illuminating as a 'stage-setter'. S. Cronin, *The McGarrity Papers* (Tralee 1972) is invaluable for the Irish-American side of events. F. Pakenham (Lord Longford), *Peace by Ordeal* (1935) deservedly remains the standard analysis of the complex Treaty negotiations of 1921. C. Younger, *Ireland's Civil War* (1968; paperback 1970) is recommended particularly for the military picture.

The essays in F. MacManus (ed.) *The Years of the Great Test, 1926–39* (Cork 1967) are of varying interest and importance. *Saorstát Éireann: Official Handbook 1932* surveys informatively the Irish Free State in its first decade of existence and has a period flavour. G. F. Hand's introduction to the *Report of the Irish Boundary Commission 1925* (Shannon 1969) skilfully elucidates a complex topic: the same writer deals in detail with Eoin MacNeill's part in the business in F. X. Martin and F. J. Byrne (eds) *The Scholar Revolutionary* (Irish University Press, Shannon 1973). D. W. Harkness, *The Restless Dominion* (1969) is a full-length study of the Irish Free State's role in the evolving British Commonwealth. Early studies of the state's political development include N. Mansergh, *The Irish Free State: its government and politics* (1934) and D. O'Sullivan's partisan *The Irish Free State and its Senate* (1940). M. Manning makes a thorough study of *The Blueshirts* (Dublin, 1970). The most comprehensive account of the I.R.A. is J. Bowyer Bell, *The Secret Army* (1970) which carries the story of the organisation up to the split in 1969–70. My own brief survey, 'The New IRA, 1925–62' is in T. D. Williams (ed.) *Secret Societies* (Dublin 1973).

K. B. Nowlan and T. D. Williams (eds), *Ireland in the War Years and After, 1939–51* (Dublin 1969) has some excellent essays and includes my 'The Irish Party System 1938–51'. The most exhaustive treatment of the 'mother-and-child scheme' episode is in J. H. Whyte, *Church and State in Modern Ireland 1923–70* (Dublin 1971). For developments in foreign policy in the late 1950s and early 1960s see C. Cruise O'Brien's entertaining *To Katanga and Back* (1962; paperback 1965) and the same author's 'Ireland in International Affairs', in O. Dudley Edwards (ed.) *Conor Cruise O'Brien Introduces Ireland* (1969): the latter book contains valuable essays on the Ireland of the 1960s.

There are numerous specialist studies for our period. Among the best books on politics are B. Chubb's informative and analytical *The Government and Politics of Ireland* (1970); M. Manning's concise *Irish Political Parties* (Dublin 1972); J. L. McCracken's most useful *Representative Government in Ireland 1919–48* (1958); C. O'Leary's history of the electoral system to 1959, *The Irish Republic and its experiment with P.R.* (Notre Dame, Indiana 1961); and B. Farrell's discussion of the power style of successive heads of government since independence, *Chairman or Chief* (Dublin 1971). The fortunes (or lack of them!) of the extra-parliamentary left are ably discussed by D. Nevin, 'Radical Movements in the Twenties and Thirties' in T. D. Williams (ed.) *Secret Societies* (Dublin 1973). For the origin and development of the Labour Party, see A. Mitchell, *Labour in Irish Politics, 1890–1930* (Irish University Press, Shannon, 1974).

The last chapter of L. Cullen, *An Economic History of Ireland since 1660* (1972) provides a sketch of the economy since independence, but the major work here is J. Meenan's admirable *The Irish Economy since 1922* (1970). The most important aspect of the economy is dealt with in R. D. Crotty's masterly *Irish Agricultural Production: Its Volume and*

Structure (Cork 1966). T. K. Whitaker's report on *Economic Development* (Dublin 1958) is obviously a seminal document.

C. Arensberg and S. T. Kimball, *Family and Community in Ireland* (2nd ed., Cambridge, Mass. 1968) is a classic anthropological study. B. Ó Cuív (ed.) *A View of the Irish Language* (Dublin 1969) and S. Ó Tuama (ed.) *The Gaelic League Idea* (Cork 1972) are full of interest. For education in general see T. J. McElligott, *Education in Ireland* (Dublin 1966). C. Brady, *Guardians of the Peace* (Dublin 1974) is the first full-length study of the Garda Síochána. The last section of D. Miller, *Church, State and Nation in Ireland 1898–21* (Dublin 1973) whets the appetite for J. H. Whyte's excellent *Church and State in Modern Ireland 1923–70* (Dublin 1971). *The Formulation of Irish Foreign Policy* (Dublin 1973) is comprehensively treated by P. Keatinge.

Northern Ireland

Pre-1969 studies include D. P. Barritt and C. F. Carter, *The Northern Ireland Problem* (1962); T. Wilson (ed.), *Ulster under Home Rule* (1955); K. E. Isles and N. Cuthbert, *An Economic Survey of Northern Ireland* (Belfast 1957); and a then fresh perspective from an 'outsider', M. W. Heslinga. *The Irish Border as a Cultural Divide* (Assen, Netherlands 1962).

Since the 'troubles' began, there has been a flow of publications, many of them 'instant' and partisan. Lack of space precludes any discussion of the literature here but the reader is referred to T. W. Moody, *The Ulster Question 1603–1973* (Cork 1974), a useful brief survey which clarifies the main developments of the crisis and provides a carefully-arranged bibliography.

Perhaps the following deserve special mention: R. Rose, *Governing without consensus* (1971); I. Budge and C. O'Leary, *Belfast, approach to crisis: a study of Belfast politics, 1603–1970* (1973); R. Harris, *Prejudice and tolerance in Ulster* (Manchester 1972); D. M. Akenson, *Education and enmity: the control of schooling in Northern Ireland* (1973); Liam de Paor, *Divided Ulster* (1970); and *The Ulster debate: report of a study group of the Institute for the Study of Conflict* (1972. Papers by J. C. Beckett and others). Of particular interest are the not dissimilar reflections of two Southern political intellectuals on the implications of the troubles for Ireland as a whole: G. FitzGerald, *Towards a New Ireland* (1972) and C. C. O'Brien, *States of Ireland* (1972).

Index

(*Note:* N.I. = Northern Ireland)